My Hurt Ta
Pain Motivated Me

Josias Jean Pierre

Dedication

This book is dedicated to all those facing life's challenges and feeling overwhelmed by the weight of their struggles. To those who feel like giving up, this book is a reminder that just because things look like defeat does not mean you are defeated.

This book is for those who feel like they don't have the strength or voice to keep going, speaking, and fighting. It is a testament to the resilience and determination of the human spirit and a reminder that even in the face of adversity, it is possible to persevere.

This book is a tribute to all those who are facing the storms of life and feeling like there is no way out. It is a message of hope and encouragement, telling them they are not alone and their struggles are a testament to their strength and courage.

So, to everyone who is feeling lost, alone, or hopeless, this book is dedicated to you. It is a reminder that you have the power to endure, overcome, and emerge victorious.

Acknowledgment

With gratitude and reverence, I acknowledge the supreme being, Lord and Savior, Jesus Christ, who guides and blesses us every step of the way.

My beloved wife, Areale Jean-Pierre, stands by me as a source of love, support, and strength. I am grateful for her presence in my life.

Besides, I acknowledge my father, Josue Jean-Pierre, and mother, Venese Jean-Pierre.

My brothers, Ernst Jean-Pierre, Jonatthan Jean-Pierre, Jovens Jean-Pierre, Sadrack Emmanuel Jean-Pierre, Jephtey Jean-Pierre, and Wisly Raymond. I am grateful for their presence in my life and our shared memories.

Lastly, I would like to acknowledge my mentors, Rashad Norris and Sean Goode, who have significantly shaped my life and guided me toward my goals. I am forever grateful for their wisdom, guidance, and support.

Contents

In a world where there's chaos and mixed messages, the main questions that we find asking ourselves are, *why me? Why God? Why is this happening? What did I do?* A lot of times, we will find ourselves asking questions because of the unknown. The fork of life hits the road, and we don't know what to do but go straight into panic mode. It's easier to look at the negative than it is to look at the positive.

The media is full of negative messages, our music is full of negative messages, and social media is full of negative messages, so it makes sense how mentally we think of the worst in the midst of the worst and not think of the best in the midst of the worst. We gravitated to a culture that has depicted our culture and identity, where it has played a part in who we are. When the setbacks of life hit, it becomes easy to throw in the towel and not see a way out. It's easy to play the victim role instead of seeing it in a champion role.

It's easy to take defeat as an answer when things are hitting rock bottom instead of seeing victory in the midst of what is happening. It's easy to look at the things going on in life and say this is over instead of seeing what is going on in life to figure out what is being taught in this season or this chapter. We often want to reap the fruits of things but fail to realize that the seed has to be planted first. The last thing to grow on a tree is the fruit. In the midst of planting seeds that will produce good fruit, there will be trials and tribulations that will try to stop you from producing positive fruits. It's up to us to make sure how we respond to life situations and ensure that it is not a response of defeat but a response of an overcomer.

A negative mindset will give negative responses, and an overcomer mindset will give overcomer responses. There are two fuels, the fuel of overcoming and defeat. Depending where your mindset stands will determine where your energy will gravitate toward when things in life get difficult and out of hand. In this book, the author shares his life story from powerless to powerful, from victim to victor, from brokenness to healing, and from defeat to overcomer.

The author had all odds thrown against him due to his conditions at birth when diagnosed with epilepsy. Over and over again, Josias will find himself back in the hospital day by day, week by week, due to this fight with epilepsy. Having to face a big father wound when his father told him at the age of five to never call him dad, as he's not his dad, but asked to call him pastor. He grew up with this rejection and the feeling of neglect, aching for a father's role and guidance. The absence of his father in his life played a role in his performance. Because of the pain that was taking place, Josias found himself causing drama and hurting others to say I need help without saying I need help. Establishing relationships was something that he couldn't do. He was searching for who he truly was in this world. When there's an absent parent at home, it can cause damage, which can cause damage to others. The void of a parent can have a long-lasting effect on a child. Even though it may not be immediate, it will reflect over time.

Josias was also an individual with special needs who had an IEP (Individual Education Plan) and was told by educators to throw in the towel because of his lack of understanding. He was told that his dreams of being an influencer and being someone of impact would never take place because of the limitations that educators and peers had seen in his life. People had seen limitations, but Josias eventually started seeing the obstacles he was facing as an opportunity for something better.

At times, he felt like his existence was an accident, but deep inside, he believed he was here for a purpose. Everyone was counting Josias out because he wasn't deemed *normal* because he had an unseeable disability. Josias had to face the issues of school and home problems while trying to manage and figure out where he belonged in the midst of what he was going through. At some point, Josias started to feel depressed and didn't feel like there was much for him in this world because of the treatment he was getting at both home and school. He started to believe that he was an accident and just here as a mistake. He had to witness domestic violence at home, seeing his mother get beaten by a man who deemed was not his father, but truly he is his father, to going to school trying to focus while in the back of his mind, he is wondering if his mother is okay.

Josias was impacted so much by these life events that he started to do things to avoid the giant that he had to face either at home or school. Josias knew that he needed some assistance to navigate through life and to have a mentor who would show him what it meant to be a man of valor and a man of integrity. After hours and hours of fasting and praying, Rashad Norris came into Josias's life in the 8th grade, taking him under his wings.

Showing Josias what it means to be a man of integrity & a man of valor. Mr. Norris has been in Josias's life for over 15 years and plays a big role in Josias's healing process. Despite the odds that were thrown against him, he had someone who was looking out for him, making sure that he was okay. Making sure that Josias had the tools that he needed to break the odds that were thrown his way.

Josias was so indulged in the pain of life that all he could do was hurt others because he was hurting. Josias didn't see that he was hurting; however, hurting people and causing drama was a way for him to say help without saying I need help. Hurt people will hurt people, but healed people heal people.

Today, Josias is a free man, a healed man, with no more bondage, no more strongholds, no more pain of the past, and he is walking truly into what God had called him to be. He is helping others to heal and grow through what they go through.

Through the impact of his mentor, Josias consistently goes down the elevator to help someone else elevate and break the cycle. Josias goes down the elevator to help someone finish the race, not give up, and just stay within the course. Through sharing his story, Josias has changed thousands of lives and shown others that there is a breakthrough, even in the midst of the chaos. From victim mentality to victor mentality, he now teaches others how to have a victorious mentality so that when life gets crazy, others will know how to respond with a victorious mentality. The work and impact that he has done throughout have gotten the eyes of many big publications. In this book, readers will know and fully understand the importance of sharing your story. Readers will understand why it's important to talk about their pain and seek the help that is needed to step into their next chapter. You'll learn how God can use what we may think was worthless and show us how it was worth it, learn how God can use what we thought was purposeless and turn it around to make it purposeful, & learn how to turn our pain into a passion so then it can create effective change.

Chapter 1 — Growing Up

Have you ever felt like the deck of cards that was given to you in life was just a sign that your whole life was going to be full of destruction? Have you ever felt like nobody understood what you were going through, and because of that, you felt like being silent was the only option for you?

Have you ever felt like if you share your story, nobody may even care about what's going on? And sometimes, you want to throw in the towel because it seems like your voice is not being valued.

For many of us, growing up was the beginning stage where our hurt began. Maybe at a young age, the deck of cards that was given to us made us believe this is what life is going to be about. You tried to understand what happened, but because you didn't understand what happened, it made you believe this was just it for you.

Maybe you were settled with what was happening and took it day by day with a smile that you knew was fake but told everybody else you were doing well when the question, *"How you're doing?"* was being asked. Nobody can control the deck of cards that was given to us, but we can control the deck of cards we choose to carry along. Just because we grew up in a certain environment, it does not mean that we have to stay in that environment. Whatever obstacle life throws at us, it does not mean that it's the final message of our lives. How we start doesn't determine the final chapters of our lives. Sometimes in life, we have this belief because it happened to me; this is how it's going to be carried down the bloodline. Because of that, our response could be, "This is what I know, and I am going to live a life based on what I know." Childhood hurt is something that has to be dealt with and talked about.

In America, we have been taught to be strong as men and taught that emotions can't show as men. There has been a stigma put behind our backs as people, especially black boys/men, that indicates that you're not manly if you don't fit certain things that society has deemed a requirement. What if I told you those stigmas that America has portrayed about our very own selves are inaccurate? What if I told you that America is providing a false identity of who we are, and they just want to shun us?

I remember growing up hearing the sentence from a family member, *"I don't care if you died."* That sentence played over and over in my head every time. This was a hurt of mine that I couldn't let go of, and I couldn't truly deal with it because I started to feel like nobody cared. I started to feel like I was all alone, and it was just me going through this misery. I started to feel like I was a nobody in the eyes of my family. I remember hearing those words from those who were so close to me and abused me with their words, and it got me to a dark moment in life where I just couldn't focus. I couldn't live life because my mind was so focused on the hurt of home situations that impacted my performance in school. In school, nobody knew why I was the way I was or knew what was really going on.

Home has been called several times due to my behavior, but even with the calls that were being made, it didn't help what was playing in my head over and over again. When tears were shedding from my eyes, all I heard was, *"You're a boy, and boys don't cry. Why are you crying for? Who touched you? Nobody beat you; you shouldn't be crying. Suck it up! You're not a baby. If you don't stop crying, I will give you something to cry about."*

Some of us may have heard these sentences being said to us when we're feeling down or feeling like we're not being heard. If you haven't heard these sentences, imagine hearing these sentences over and over again. Crying and aching to be heard. Crying for acceptance and belonging. Crying for attention as a young boy because you didn't get that attention at all that was needed. How do you cope with feelings if nobody doesn't want to guide you to cope with what you're feeling? How are you supposed to walk free when it feels like freedom will never be here for you? I couldn't dwell right on the issue because I was afraid of the consequences that would take place if I just talked about the pain. I was afraid of what it could be because I didn't want to be separated from my family.

While I smiled along and went through the motions of happiness, it was a dark spot on the inside that held me back from believing I wasn't destined for anything good. It was the brokenness inside that made me believe this was it for me. I was the only one in my family diagnosed with epilepsy and a learning disability.

I was the only one in my family whom you could say was different, and because of that difference, I was treated differently. Because of that, depression hovered over me at a young age, leading to the youth and young adult stages. Nobody knew I was depressed because I played it so well. It was something I was fighting, and nobody even knew that I was fighting it.

I couldn't talk about it. Talking about depression was as if it was a joke, like kids can't struggle or go through anything. Being uncomfortable and feeling uncomfortable was overlooked as if the elders could only tell you how you feel, and that's it. It was as if your experience wasn't really an experience because you shouldn't feel that as a young child. The mentality of the adults about kids growing up was, *"You are just a kid. You don't know what hurt and pain feel like. You don't know what struggle feels like. You're just a kid, and kids are good at being kids."* Well, this kid, growing up, doesn't know how to face the pain of hate that has been built inside me for a long time. The more my hurt was silenced, it turned into a giant that I didn't know how to manage.

I grew up hating my dad. When I was five years old, I remember he looked my brothers and me in the eye and told us, *"Never call me dad; I'm not your dad."* What kid wants to hear that? Throughout the years, when folks asked me where was my father? My immediate response has always been, I don't have one.

At a young age, part of me was broken and searching for a father's love and guidance. I grew up in the church, but I didn't feel like the church would understand why I was this violent. It was hard for me to connect to God, the father, when I couldn't even connect to my earthly father. It was hard for me to believe that God was a good father when I didn't even see one in front of me. Because of this hurt, I became a private person and hurt others because I was hurt. My hurt from neglect, abandonment, and rejection overwhelmed me to the point where I could feel alone even amid company. Talking about your hurt to those who hurt you was disrespectful in their eyes. If you dare tell them how you truly feel, it's as if you were attacking them. My voice couldn't be heard, and because of that, I hurt others to be heard without saying I needed help.

For a long time, I was silenced by those who were so close to me that I didn't know how to talk about my pain to those who were not so close. I had to witness fourteen years of domestic violence and witness a broken home which led me to have a broken soul. All I wanted was a good role model of a man and how that should look like. I knew I didn't want to do what society has deemed a man or what a black man is.

I knew I didn't like what the media was portraying about manhood, so I was on a search looking for role models, leaders, and potential father figures in my life. All I wanted was the embracement and to hear from my dad, *"I love you & I'm proud of you."* This hurt affected me so much that I tried to fill this emptiness inside with everything else, but nothing wouldn't fill that void. I used violence to express the hurt, but it led to more hurt. I started watching pornography to fulfill something at the moment, but I was still hurt in the long run. Moment satisfaction can still lead to long-term destruction. Just because it felt good at the moment, it doesn't mean it will feel good in the long haul. I didn't know where to go or to whom I could express my hurts and emotions. It was okay to go to the doctor to get checked, but it wasn't okay to see a therapist. Therapy wasn't something that was part of our community, and it was looked at and viewed as something so bad if you went to therapy.

Therapy in my community wasn't accepted, and for some reason, it was shunned for one to go to therapy. Because of that, I tried to figure out this hurt on my own. I tried to figure out the why's behind all this because I wasn't grasping not one reason at the moment why I am in what I am in. There were times that the home issues I was facing would be playing in my head all over again as if this was going to be my reality.

The only time I smiled so genuinely was when I was not around those who were supposed to be close to me. The only time where I felt more at peace was when I was not home. Everything is home training. But when you don't have that home training or positive influence, then what do you do? When you don't have that guidance, where do you go? When you feel so disconnected from the ones, who are supposed to be your family, who do you look up to next?

I knew what I had seen on TV was not going to be an option or even a thought of last resort because I knew there had to be something better than what I was seeing. I knew not all black people are like what society has shown; however, where are they? I remember my senior year in high school, I got up and gave a speech to my classmates in the cafeteria a couple of days before we actually sealed the deal for graduation.

I was looking at the crowd, and I was looking at my mom, and I started sharing this hurt with my peers with tears rolling down my eyes, telling them, my mom is my mom, and my mom is my dad. One of the questions my peers have always asked me was, *"Where is your dad?"* Since I was a kid, my response was, I don't have one. This man, who is supposedly my father, told us never to call him dad because he's not our dad.

I woke up every day believing that I was fatherless and this man had no reason to talk to me because he was not my dad. My biggest hurt was yearning for a father's love and guidance. My biggest hurt was the fact that I was the only one with a learning disability in my family, and I was always told that I would never become anything because of my disability. I don't recall not one time when I was told by my family that they believed I could do it. I don't recall one time I was told anything that said you can do this, and you can do that. The only time I was told that I needed or could do this was when they wanted me to do something on their behalf. But when it comes to basic home training and basic home functions, I was never shown that because my family believed my disability of epilepsy was the reason why I couldn't do X, Y, & Z. My disability was hidden, and you wouldn't know I had a disability unless I told you I had one. If I didn't tell you I had a learning disability, you would never know that. The only see-able disability you would have seen was the fact that I stuttered so much and had issues annunciating my words. Growing up, I didn't have people close to me speaking life over me but instead always declaring negative affirmations.

The lack of positive affirmations led me to run away from home twice. The first time was in middle school, and the other was in high school. I was so tired of the negativity going on at home and tired of the treatment that I felt like I was not a part of the family. You would have thought I was the stepchild in the family because the treatment was so different compared to the treatment my brothers were getting. My brothers were given the tools and access to learning home stuff while I was told that I was not able to do anything because of my disability. When in reality, I could do the same functions as my brothers. But because of my learning disability, I was always told I couldn't do this and couldn't do that. Because of that, I was never allowed to learn or even get my feet wet. The second time I ran from home was when I was in high school. At this point, the hurt increased measurably. The hurt increased to the point where I truly believed that God had made a mistake putting me in this family. There were times when I asked God, why did you put me in this family? Why am I here? Why am I going through this? Why am I facing this? This must be an accident that I am here! There's no purpose for me here.

My family doesn't believe in me, my peers are making fun of me because of my lack of comprehension, and teachers are telling me to give up and throw in the towel due to them not being adequately trained to work with those with special needs. I had so many questions with no answers that I chose to run away from home for a couple of days while my family was panicking, trying to figure out if I was okay.

I can recall being at my friend's house, and my cell phone was blowing up with calls from my family, and I didn't even answer. I told my mom that I would be out for one day, but she usually hears from me about updates. At this point, there weren't any updates. One day passed, and they didn't hear from me. The second day passed, and they didn't hear from me. On the third day, I went home, and the first thing that took place were questions. The only reason *why* questions were being asked was that my friend and his mom were at the house. One thing I knew was that if my friend's mom didn't come into the house, questions wouldn't be the first thing asked. The moment when my friend and his mom left the house was when the spanking came. I got the spanking of my life. While I'm being spanked, I'm being asked why I did what I did. And the spanking continued without even giving me the opportunity to answer anything.

The moment where I shared the hurt that was caused at home, I was called disrespectful and told that I was lying about how I felt, as if youth shouldn't have feelings. At this point in my life, it was hurt that was built on top of more hurt, which had led to the youth stage. It was hurt that started as a kid to a hurt that leveled up with me to the youth stages. This hurt got to me so much that I attempted suicide and was done with life. Nobody knew I attempted suicide besides the ones who were there screaming *no* from the top of their lungs and did everything in their own might to hold me back from attempting suicide. I was able to break loose from them, holding me back and running toward heavy oncoming traffic, but I made it to the other side while the traffic level was heavy. I did the same action twice, and I kept making it to the other side, and I didn't understand how I made it, nor did my peers have any idea of how I made it. But they were glad I was still alive — glad that I didn't die. At the moment, I felt like death would be the best decision for me at this point since my cries couldn't be heard, my voice couldn't be heard, and the attention I needed was not there.

When I made it to the other side the second time in full heavy traffic, I then had to question *why I was not dead. Why am I here? Why? Why? Why?* I remember a friend by the name of Calvin Gray had invited me to go to his church called Citadel. A church where the mission was to *"Connect people to God and develop*

11

them for influence." I remember when I walked into the church doors, I saw the mission statement posted right on the wall. While being at the church, something felt different, from walking into the building to going to the sanctuary, which was located downstairs.

I remember the youth pastor, Pastor Matt, preaching about not being an accident and being here for a purpose. And he went on and said, *"Some of you had asked God why you're in the family you're in. Why are you facing what you're facing? And I'm here to tell you that you're in the family you're in for a purpose and for a reason. It's not an accident that you're alive, and it's not an accident that you're born in the family that you're in. One thing I do know is that God can turn things around for his glory."*

The message was for me, and it was the word where I believed that the Why-question was answered at that moment. Pastor Matt said, *"If you're here and you need God to move in your life, and you're on the edge of just breaking, come and let us pray for you. You don't have to leave these doors the same way you came in."* While it was my first time in this church, I went up, and the pastor looked at me and started prophesying over my life.

He went on and said, *"You have a story. You're going to be that voice for your generation, and you can't give up. The enemy will attack you because the calling of your life is that strong. You will overcome whatever it is you're going through, and you will have a message that will change your school and change your generation. Hang in there."* When he was telling me those words, it still didn't make sense whatsoever what he was saying, but I just received it and took it with little belief. It sounded good, but I wasn't quite sure. The whole week it sat with me with what the pastor prophesied over my life. The next following week, Calvin Gray told me that he wanted me to know that there was a safe space around him and that he felt there was something heavy that I was going through that I needed to let go of in order for me to elevate to the next level. He continued and told me, *"Josias, I'm your bro! I am going to be here for you, and I got your back. You're not alone, my brother!"* The more I kept sharing with him what I was facing and going through, the freer I felt. The more we went through the process together, the more hurt on the inside started to release, and freedom was coming in. It wasn't an overnight freedom, but it was a process. The glow was different, the smile was different, and I started to see the prophecy manifesting in full effect. I started going to this church with Calvin, and I found myself drawing closer to God.

One following week, the pastor was talking about ministry in the school and bringing friends with you to come to church. I did just that. Slowly but surely, the students at my school started coming to church with me on a consistent basis. The numbers started increasing with Tyee High School students coming to the church. They started sharing the encounter that they had, which brought more people to come and get this same encounter. At the moment, the hurt never made sense, but behind the hurt, there was a lesson that I grasped. The hurt taught me five things which will be listed below:

Talk About Your Hurt, Don't Hold It In

Our hurt has to be addressed at the moment and before it's too late. My hurt increased from when I was a kid, which led to youth, and by the time the hurt increased and leveled up to my youth days, it birthed a giant that I was not willing to face. Our hurt is not meant to be kept, and even when we feel like someone will not understand, just know that there's someone out there that truly does understand. Many of us had let the hurt of our youth go with us to our different chapters of life when it wasn't supposed to come to those different chapters of life.

When I say chapters, I am referring to our age. The older we get, that's a new chapter of our life. It's okay to say I'm not okay, but it's not okay to stay not being okay. You don't have to tell everyone what it is you're going through, but you have to talk to someone about the very thing you're going through. There's freedom in talking about your hurt and sharing your story.

Freedom doesn't just apply to you but to others around you who can receive hope just by hearing your story. I didn't know at the time what was going on and how things would turn out. But the more I started sharing my hurt and my story with others, the more hope others around me started to receive. I didn't even know there were people who were in my shoes because they seemed so happy. While they seemed so happy, I seemed so broken. They smiled, but I was really hurting and not smiling. The moment I shared my hurt and became free from the very thing holding me back, my smile became more genuine, and a surmount of peace hovered over me that I couldn't even explain.

The more I shared my hurt and my story, the more people started talking about their hurt and felt hopeful because they saw that they were not by themselves in this fight. Your story can be a jewel to someone else. One soul trash is another soul treasure, and just know there are jewels in your story that can be treasured by someone else. The second thing I learned is listed below.

There's An Expiration Date

We always hear the phrase, *"There's light at the end of the tunnel. Keep staying the course; hang in there."* Those phrases have been some of the common phrases when it comes to letting people know what they face is not permanent; it's temporary. Everything in life has an expiration date, including the hurts we are in. It might feel like it's permanent because of the length of time the hurt stayed there. To heal, it's going to require us to take action for the healing process. Don't ever think what you're in is the final message of your life but look at what you're in as there's going to be a powerful message once you break through for your breakthrough. There are going to be times in life when we are going to believe that we will never get through it because we've been in the same area for weeks, months, or even years. Despite how long it takes, it's not going to be forever, even if it feels like it's forever. The race to victory is not going to be easy; it's going to be a process, and we won't be victorious with a mentality that is defeated. Defeated mindsets give defeated responses.

Overcoming mindsets give overcoming responses. When we understand that the storm and trials, and tribulations that we face are there to build us up and push us toward the better good, we will then keep fighting this fight with a mentality of a champion. When I realized that I was stepping closer to my freedom and being an overcomer, I then realized I was free from this hurt, but the hurt is now doing something different.

It's creating lessons and messages for others. It's giving people the tools to be equipped to face it till they make it and not fake it until they make it. It's giving the people the tools to understand what they're in is preparing for something better. You may not know exactly when the better is going to come, but it's going to be better. The hurt might expire, but the motivation behind the hurt will become the fire that will elevate you toward your purpose. The third thing I learned is listed below.

Message Behind The Mess

We all have a commission in this world. We all are destined with something that will leave positive impacts when we step foot. The mess in life may not have to be a part of your purpose, but it can be used for a powerful message. I am a firm believer that all things work for the good. We may not see the good at the moment because, at the moment, what's going through the mind is, how can I get out of this? I want this to be over with already. What's going through our mind is not thinking about the good but literally how much hurt we are facing in the midst of this mess that we are in.

One thing I have learned is that the mess in life creates a powerful message in our lives. The mess in life builds things in us that can be used to build others who are attached to our lives. What we are in is not for us, but it's for someone else who needs to hear how we made it through. I could recall the day when I was delivered from this hurt and how quickly I was used to sharing this very hurt with others without knowing that the audience had thoughts of committing suicide and had father-related issues. I was walking through my college campus, and there was a sign where a camp was looking for counselors to be a part of the summer staff and counsel different kids each week. It was 2013 when I was a counselor at Camp Berachah, now known as Black Diamond Camps, in Auburn, WA. I was doing an overnight camp for high school students for one week, and they didn't want to be a part of it. They were at camp for the sole purpose of just having fun and doing what they wanted to do, but nothing more than that. This camp is a Bible-believing camp, which means that we will share the gospel of Christ with these kids. The more I tried to share, the more they were not willing to listen and be disengaged.

There was a point when I got all the kids' attention, and I shared my story of attempted suicide and my father's wound story. Every kid in the cabin started shedding tears. I was responsible for ten kids, and out of them, seven had plans of committing suicide. And all ten had issues with their fathers. We all sat there, shedding tears and sharing our own stories, and the message that they left before the week was over was hope, assurance, and victory. When they came to camp, their message was hopeless, pointless, not valued, and confusing. Because I shared my story and went to a vulnerable position with the high schoolers, they were able to leave with assurance and hope that they would get through this. They were able to leave with the confidence that they would step into their breakthrough. Before that week was over, the ten kids who didn't want anything to do with camp now are able to love camp because their freedom happened just by sharing my story.

Don't ever think there's no message behind the mess you're in. Don't ever believe that what you went through could not do anything to anybody else. Your story is a helpline to someone else's victory. Just because you may not think it's not valuable doesn't mean that it has no value. Your story can be the message that someone needs to hear.

There's beauty behind our story, and God can use what we may think is worthless and show us how it was worth it. God can use what we may think was purposeless and turn it around to be purposeful. You're needed in a time like this, and it's not the time to be silent about your message. This is the time to be vocal about your message so others can be motivated, empowered, and equipped to stay on the race and fight the good fight. The fourth thing I learned is listed below.

Testimony Behind The Test

Whatever brings you closer to your goals and dreams is not your enemy but your friend. Whatever pushes you for the better is not your enemy but your friend. During a test, the teacher is always silent and may not help when help feels needed. In life, one of the purposes of the test is not to punish us but to show us what we really have on the inside. It's to show us what we truly believe about ourselves. We will never know what we believe about ourselves until the storms of life come. When the storm comes, we will see what's in us come out of us. The test is there to build us up, but in the process of elevation, things must die so we can increase to the next level. Things must decrease so we can increase.

I truly believe what I was going through and facing in life was preparing me for my message and also for a powerful testimony. I could've _____ should've   _____   would've _____, but God stepped in and did something different. My story could've ended at 15 when I attempted suicide. My story should've ended at birth when I was pronounced dead by doctors because of epilepsy. My story would've ended when I was a kid and a neighbor pulled his gun out and pointed toward me while I was outside playing, and my mother was inside the house sleeping. But because of God, I don't look at what I have been through. Because of God, the test and trials that I had faced prepared me to travel and equip other people who may have faced what I was facing. Because of God, my story has transformed the lives of many youths, young adults, and adults to have hope and reassurance to keep on staying the course even when it feels like there's no way out. Whatever test you're in, it's there to build you up and launch you to something better and bigger than yourself. Your testimony is not for you, but it's for someone else. You are a living miracle that has a testimony that can shift lives for the good.

Your testimony is meant to be shared, and behind every test of life, there's a message that needs to be testified on how you made it through. Despite the hurt and the wounds of life, understand there's a purpose and a message through it all. We may not understand the trials and tribulations we're in, but we can know one thing, God can turn it around for good. The fifth thing I learned is listed below.

Ministry Behind The Misery

The last thing I've learned is that behind the miseries could birth a ministry. When I say ministry, I am not referring to any religious activities, but I am referring to the commission that is set for all of us. I am referring to our purpose as to why we are still breathing. If you're breathing, it's because there's more in you. The miseries of life have one end goal, which is to shape us toward that purpose. Mold us toward that purpose. And equip us toward that purpose. The only way the miseries of life make us fall backward and not go forward is if we allow it. The way we could allow it is by our response to the storm. What we believe about ourselves will determine how we will respond in the midst of the storm. The affirmations we declare over our lives will determine how we fight in the middle of the storm. It's not if the storm will come, but it's when it does come; how do we respond? I realized behind all the miseries I had faced in my life was birthing a passion in me for lost souls.

I realize behind all the things that I went through in my life motivated me to go down the elevator and pick someone else up with me. Behind the misery is a passion that is birthing in you. That passion could be what you're commissioned to do in this world. I didn't know why many things happened the way they happened in my life. But I do know one thing: everything I have encountered in life has created opportunities to walk into my purpose of mentoring others to become an overcomer, think like a champion, and fight like a champion.

When going through the miseries, it didn't feel good; however, bouncing back from the misery showed me how many people were in my shoes and needed help to get through what I bounced back from. You're in what you're in for a purpose. It's not an accident. When you're facing what you're facing, don't let your feelings have a voice in what could happen next. Feelings fluctuate; if you move by how you feel, you can move in the wrong direction. When things seem crazy in your life, and you don't understand the why behind it, just know there's a purpose behind it. The purpose is not for you, but it's for someone else who needs to be equipped and shaped by your story, by your ministry, and by your testimony.

When the pot is hot, something is cooking. When the storms of your life seem hot, something is cooking. The recipes in the cooking will be added by how you respond to that situation. I remember when things were hot in my life. I was bringing recipes of destruction based on how I was responding to the storms I was in.

It wasn't until I adopted the mentality of an overcomer that I started speaking victory over my situations, a breakthrough for the storms that I was facing, and finding healing for me. When I adopted the mentality of an overcomer, things were changing for the good. It started changing because what I placed in the driver's seat was God. I just believed God in his word and that he would do what he said he was going to do. Whatever you're going through, understand that if there's a will, there's a way. Understand, if God is in the driver's seat, he will fight your battles, turn what it is you're going through, and use that to commission you toward your purpose.

Chapter 2 — Masking My Pain

One of the biggest things people told me growing up was I do way too much and don't understand why I am never home. People will even say, you're Jamaican with five jobs. Why can't you stick to one job? Even though they were correct that I was never home, nobody knew why I was never home beside the people in my circle. My own family would see me leave the house and don't even know where I was going. I was so closed off from everybody that I was afraid of opening up to people.

I was tired of being shut down. I told myself I would deal with this by myself. I hated that my voice couldn't be heard, my cries couldn't be acknowledged, and people assumed I was lying when talking about how I was feeling. Nobody didn't show me the game plan on how to overcome, how to bounce back, and how to recover from the hurt; they just told me to hang in there.

As if I knew what hanging in there meant. I moved independently for a long time; I was used to doing things by myself. I was afraid of opening up because there was a trend of people not believing my hurt and pain. Some people thought I over-exaggerated things and just laughed when I was talking about the very hurt I was dealing with. People wanted me to be so present in the moment and failed to realize I didn't have the strength to be present in the moment. At the moment, I was hurt, wounded, bruised, depressed, fighting a mental battle that many did not even see. I didn't know how to face it till I made it because, throughout the years, I was told I had to fake it till I made it.

The hurt from being a child increased over time, which led me to be quiet about the very thing I was facing. People thought I was so happy because I was smiling and laughing with them, but they never knew there was a battle that I was facing, which almost took me out for the count. People saw me doing a lot of things, and because I didn't look like I was struggling, they didn't believe that I was struggling. Not everyone who smiles is really happy. And not everyone who looks happy is *really* happy. I've been told to fake it till I make it for so long that I became very good at putting on a show hoping that I will make it.

Throughout the years, I masked the pain because silence was all that I knew. Throughout the years, I didn't know how to establish a strong, healthy relationship because toxicity was attached to me. I would go to church and put on praise, but the praise wasn't even genuine. I would go to church and serve, but the service that I was doing was not unto God; it was unto man. I was getting burned out, and I responded with frustration and anger when people told me that I needed to do X, Y, & Z. My response to everyone who kept on asking if I could assist in different areas was, *"Why can't you do it yourself? You got two hands and two feet. Why don't you want to do it on your own?"* I was getting offended when people tried to pass the buck down to me because they didn't want to do it. I was known as the individual who stayed in his lane. I was good at masking the hurt, but eventually, the hurt led to more hurt and being more distant. I was doing everything just to get my mind off the battles I was told to be silent about.

Since therapy wasn't normalized in my community, I had to play a role, so others won't know I was hurting. I had to play a role so others couldn't see that I was really broken. I had to play a role just so I didn't have to face the war in my own backyard. It was hard to talk about the pain to church people because they were so quick to tell me what I was feeling and encountering was the devil, not God. They were so quick to rebuke me but not quick to help me when I needed help. The church was quick to judge my downfalls but not quick to provide assistance when needed. The church was good at bringing the church cliches that I started acting like the church, but it never was the church. I started catching up on how they do things while they were masking up their own pain. When people asked me how I was doing, I quickly said, *"I am blessed and highly favored. Praise God. Amen!"* I was good at doing the church traditions and saying the church cliches. But at the same time, I wasn't really blessed and highly favored. I was really broken and looking for desperate help. It was hard for me to connect to God that the people were talking about in church when the actions didn't represent the God that these people were talking about. It was hard for me not to differentiate people and God together because what people were reaping in the church looked like what the world was reaping, and they were a part of the world.

I went to church because it was a thing of my family to go to church. If you're in the house, you're going to church. No if's or but's about it. If you're living under the roof, you're going despite what you feel and what you're going through. The church was like a box that was checked that you went to church but nothing else. I can recall seeing everyone else singing, shouting, screaming, running around the church, and having a *praise break* because that was a part of the traditions of how the church was doing it. Because of my hurt and pain being neglected in the church, which was supposed to be the hospital for the broken, I had no other choice but to mask my pain. The place that was supposed to be there for the broken wasn't really there for the broken. The place that was supposed to be there for the hopeless wasn't really there for the hopeless. The place that was supposed to be there for those who are in the last straw before throwing in the towel wasn't there for them. I was in the presence of a company and still felt alone in the company. I was told to hush and not say anything about my hurt and what was going on because it's not everyone's business.

The question arose in my head, how am I supposed to walk in freedom if I have to be silent about the very thing that is killing me inside? How much longer am I supposed to fake it when it feels like I am on the edge of throwing in the towel? How much longer am I supposed to water down my feelings just so people can't be exposed to the hurt and pain that they have caused me? How much longer do I have to shed tears at night, fighting every day while trying to be free? Just because I wasn't locked in chains and whips, it does not mean that my mental state wasn't. Every day it was a constant battle with myself. Josias, you're this; Josias, you're that. No, Josias, you're not this; you're not that. Have you ever had those voices in your head which made you question a lot about yourself? Have you ever had those voices in your head, and you just pondered on the worst things as if it was true? Masking my pain held me back from accessing true freedom. The best freedom anyone could ever have is the freedom of the mind. And if our minds aren't free from the very thing that is holding us back from elevating and growing, we will keep on masking the pain, market a fake version of who we really are, just so we can be accepted in the eyes of those who may not even accept us if the real us came out.

Until I dealt with the giants in my closet, I was able to remove the mask I had been wearing for a long time. What pain are you masking that you want to be free from? What is in your closet that you're not willing to battle? What is in your life that you're being silent about due to the message of the masses or the message of people who are close to you? The moment where I took the mask off, I was able to walk into my authentic self and really see who I really was. Taking the mask off was not easy, but it was a process. It was not easy because I had trust issues and couldn't trust anybody. The vulnerability was not considered manly.

Because of that, when it was time to be vulnerable and share my story, I always said no and accepted the pain because of the fear of the unknown. I have always said no because I didn't want people to enter my real world to really hear what was really going on with me outside the four walls of school and church. You can't expect me to share my deepest secrets; when I did try to share, I was told to be quiet and not to talk about it. You can't expect me to share the pain within when I am being told to be present and fake it until you make it. I took the chance on myself one last time and shared with people who were much older than me about what I was going through. I realized that the mask can't be taken off until we talk about the hurt that we're going through.

When we talk about the very hurt that we're going through, it doesn't only free us, but it also frees others around us. It doesn't just free us, but we will be able to see that we are not alone in the storm. There are others who are also in the same storm. If we want to let go of the mask that we're used to holding onto, we have to be able to share the deepest things that nobody may even know about us.

Don't share it with anybody but share it with someone that you can trust. Matter of fact, go to a therapist and share it with them because they can help you take that mask off that has been there for a long time. Masking the pain affected different things in my life and also showed me two things which I will list below:

Identity Crisis

Masking the pain caused me to have an identity crisis where I tried to figure out who I was. I was blinded to see the potential in me because I had let life's strongholds grab me. I was so blind to see that I was someone with potential because I didn't know how to tap into my full potential. When you're hurt and full of pain, and you're told for a long time to fake it until you make it, masking the pain can become the voice of defeat over our lives.

It felt like around us was a defeat, but we weren't defeated. Outside of my success and credentials, I couldn't answer the question, Who is Josias? Without adding my accolades, I couldn't answer that question because I didn't know who I was. I was still trying to figure out who is this Josias that was created in this world. What was I commissioned to do?

For years, I was battling with my identity because I didn't feel like I had a good representation in this season of my life to get assistance for my identity. Masking the pain can lead to confusion of identity, where you will look everywhere and anywhere to figure out your identity. Some of us will look at the world for acceptance because we don't feel like we're accepted within our own community. We don't feel like we are worthy enough, so we will do whatever we can for someone to say yes, come on in. We will dehumanize ourselves just to be accepted. We will do anything to avoid the pain but fail to realize that the pain will never avoid us until we take action.

One thing about confusion, it's a spirit that should never be activated. When the spirit of confusion is manifested, the enemy will take root and feed his lies into our lives and send his traps for us to believe the very thing happening in front of our eyes is true. The enemy only tells lies when it's almost the truth. The reason why it happens when it's almost the truth is that we have planted the seed for the enemy to send his traps for us to believe it's true.

The enemy is only there to kill, steal, and destroy. He will do whatever he can so you won't tap into the very thing God has for you. I got to a point in my life where I said, *God, who am I? God, what do you have in store for me? God, why am I here? God, I am hurting to the core. I don't know who I am, and they tell me that my life is mapped into your hands. If that is true, God, please show me who I am because I don't know. Please guide me because I can no longer guide myself. God, they say my identity is in you, but I am too hurt and blind to see what that identity is. God, if you just can.... God, if you just.... God! I was tired of faking the funk, going through the motions, and the church cliches.*

I was tired of hearing about the fruits of Christ but not seeing the body manifesting the fruits of Christ. In life, the actions that people do will make you believe this is who they worship or believe. Often, that's why the people in the world have a hard time believing there's a God or that Christ is the true living God because the fruits that the church bears match the fruits the world bears. The fruit that believers bear should be different from what the world bares. It wasn't until I fully surrendered with arms wide open and gave God broken praise that I truly found my identity in him. The best praise I believe anyone can give is broken praise. The reason why that is it's because you're giving all that you got with no reserves.

You don't care what's around you or whose looking because you are in a place of desperation, and you just want a touch from God. I surrendered fully with a mustard size seed faith that God would do what he said He was going to do. The more I kept praising and crying His name out, the more I started feeling freer and freer from the very thing that was keeping me bound.

Because of the encounter that I had, I was intrigued to know Him for myself. The more I got into His word, the more things were happening for good. I started declaring and believing who God said that I was and not what the world said that I was. I started believing and declaring what God said about me and not what the world said about me. I realize in the world's identity, lies and deception is the seed that will be planted over one's life. But in God's identity, truth and life will be the only thing that will be attached no matter what the circumstance around us may look like. When the mask was removed and the veil was taken off, I had a boost of confidence that I never had. I had a peace that passed all understanding. No matter what was happening in my life, the peace I had got me to rest in God's unchanging hand and believe that he would get the glory behind all this. The second thing that was masking the pain showed me is listed below.

Lack Of Acceptance And Loving Others

When you can't love yourself, you can't love others around you. When you can't accept yourself, you can't accept others around you. It was hard for me to accept people and believe that people wanted the best for me when what was around me was *really* the worst. It was hard to believe that people were there for the long haul when people seemed to depart ways when things were getting difficult.

People started departing ways once they had been told what was *really* going on with me. I treated others the same because my hurt blinded me from seeing there were genuine people who really wanted to help. There are people who are not going to gossip about the very thing we go through but work with us to overcome it. It's hard to accept that when it was hard accepting myself. It was hard to accept that people loved me with no limitations when I didn't understand the purpose of why they loved me because I couldn't love myself. Because of the struggle of loving self and accepting self, it was hard to let people into my life.

I had walls and barriers up because of past hurt, which were triggers that were re-happening over and over again. Masking the pain blinded me from seeing my worth. It was as if every day was Halloween because a mask was always worn. The mask worn throughout the week was the mask of failure, rejection, abandonment, neglect, and depression. I felt like there weren't any choice but to carry this mask that people had told me to keep so I could make it. When truthfully, my faking has led me to attempt suicide and say I was done with life.

I didn't really accept and love myself until I realized that I was worth fighting for. I had people in my life like Rashad Norris, Sean Goode, & Jesse Parker, who had fought on my behalf in multiple ways because they believed I was worth fighting for. I remember when Norris came into my life, and he embraced me with open arms and dedicated his time to see me evolve into the best version of me. Before we departed ways or got off the phone, he always told me he loved me. People would have thought that Norris was my dad because of the love he was giving as if I was his son. I, never in my life, felt a father & son love because I didn't have that while growing up in life. It's been 15 years that strong Norris has been in my life, and we are still close; he is still there, and if need be, he will fight on my behalf because he has seen something worth fighting for. Norris showed me what it means to be a man of valor, a man of integrity, and a man of honor. He didn't just talk the talk, but he walked what he talked. His actions and his love have transformed my life for the good.

Goode showed me that it's okay to cry and it's okay to release so I can *be free.* He told me, *"It's not easy, I know. It doesn't feel good, I know. I have been in your shoes, but the best thing you can do is forgive. Forgive because if you don't forgive, you will never be free from the hurt that you have been carrying for so long. Forgive because there's no value in holding it in. Joe! You're loved, and you don't have to be someone that you're not. Be the authentic you because the authentic you is needed, not a fake version of you."*

When Goode told me that, I had tears rolling down my eyes, and he was hugging me and holding me and embracing me, and letting me know that he would always be there for me no matter what. He sees my brother and me as his own and, therefore, will go above and beyond for my brother and me no matter what. The last time I talked to Goode in person was at the MLK Jr. Rally at Garfield High School in Seattle, WA. I saw Sean and told him, *"Thank You, Thank You, Thank You, Thank You."* Thank you for being hard on me and making yourself available for my brother and me. Your presence is the reason why I am present for those in times of trouble. Your love and the fight that you did for me is the reason why I fight for others who are battling a storm that they believe they can't make it through. Thank you for making yourself available and having my brother and me cry in your arms until we couldn't cry anymore. Goode said, *"Joe, you and your brother are always welcome to cry in my arms. I love you all, and no matter what, and if you ever need that shoulder to cry on, I am here and available."*

Parker was my youth leader. Parker was someone that would give you the message raw and with no sugar-coating. He will bring a message where you can't help but take action because it was that moving. I met Parker at Citadel church when I was in high school. Parker always gave me rides home because I never had a ride home. He has always said, *"You come. I will make sure you get home."* Every time I was there, I always had a ride home. If the ride wasn't from him, it was from someone else, but he always made sure I had a ride home. While having Parker as my youth leader, the very things I would be praying about for my life, Parker would preach about that very thing, and he and I didn't even converse yet about what was going on outside the four walls. I couldn't help but go to Mr. Parker and tell him my background and the hurt I was facing. One thing he didn't do was provide scriptures. So often, the church can be so quick to give scriptures instead of being present and catering to what is going on. Mr. Parker realized that I needed someone to be present at the time, and he made sure he was always present. He made himself available and accepted me despite my flaws and my hurts; he accepted me and loved me as if I was his own.

He said something when he was preaching at the youth service, which caught my attention. He said, *"I want you all to know I will always be present for you all, and I will always love you and be present. I also want you to know that God loves you much more than anybody else who says they love you. God's love is unconditional, but human love has conditions. God's love does not have restrictions, and I want you to know that God will accept you as is and will love you as is. However, in this journey, while walking with God, you won't stay the way you are. There are those of us who feel devalued and not worthy of acceptance because of the life issues going on. There are those of us who are so hard on ourselves that we feel that a transformation can't take place. Some of us carry a mask and don't want to show our scars and wounds. You don't have to carry those scars and those wounds; God can heal you and remove the mask that you have been carrying for so long."* For some reason, that message in itself brought me to tears. While Parker called the leaders to the front, and the alter was open for anyone to come if they needed prayer while the worship team was going to continue in worship, I remember the pianist Kamaria playing the gospel song, *"Break Every Chain"* and also singing the song while she was playing it. While Parker was praying for me, all of a sudden, I felt a peace that hovered over me, which was unexplainable. The peace that I got the world didn't give it to me, nor can the world take it away. I was able to accept myself and love myself and view myself differently.

When I started to believe I was worth fighting for and started loving and accepting myself, I was able to view others differently and love others differently. Since the peace that I received was unexplainable, I wanted others to get that same peace that passed all understanding. Because of that, I was speaking life to others around me in the midst of what they were going through. I started to speak about God's identity to people compared to the world's identity. When the mask was removed, everything that was attached to me, such as depression, abandonment, neglect, rejection, etc., was also removed. When we no longer mask the pain, we will see much clearer. The voice that is being declared in the midst of the storm will be different. Before, the voice was a voice of defeat, making us believe we were defeated. But when we overcome one struggle after another, there's hope that arises and a strong belief that we can overcome whatever we are facing.

When the mask was removed, I was able to speak life where death was. When the mask was removed, I was able to speak hope to where it seemed like it was hopelessness. When the mask was removed, I was able to speak life where life needed to be. When the mask was removed, I was able to step into the possibilities that people had deemed impossible for my life. I was able to accept myself and start loving others in the same manner that I was loving myself.

When we can't accept ourselves, it will be hard to accept other people. When the mask was taken off, the veil was taken off too. I had to remove this mask that was holding me back to go after everything that God had in store for me.

What are some things that are holding us back from loving ourselves? Are we on the wayside, waiting for a change? Or are we taking action to be a part of the change we want to happen in our life?

Despite what the norms of society are and what the world says, we should know what God has for us is much more precious than what anyone else can provide. I want you to know that the masks that we have over our faces are only hiding the real beauty of us and who God created us to be. There is no benefit to the mask; therefore, we must remove the mask. The mask that we have on is only killing us and destroying everything about us where we will question our very own existence as if we're an accident and not here for a purpose.

I want to let you know that nothing about us is an accident, nothing about us is a mistake, and everything about us is attached to purpose. We're born on purpose, for a purpose, and with a purpose. We're worth fighting for; better yet, God believed and still believes that we were and are worth fighting for that He sent his son, Jesus Christ, to die on the cross because He believes we're worth that much. The mask of shame, guilt, abandonment, neglect, rejection, etc. was already covered in the cross of Calvary.

Whatever mask we put on every day to walk through society, we should understand that it's already been paid in Calvary. When God stepped in the gap, it was already finished. Because of what He has done on the cross, we have the power to be overcome by the blood of the lamb and the word of our testimony. When I tried to remove the mask by myself, it was tough. But when I let go of myself and let God take over, I was able to step into the authentic self with the power of Christ. Without Him, we are powerless, but with Him and through Him, we are made powerful. We need to grasp and know that we are made powerful in Him and through Him. When we are weak, He is strong. There is nothing too big for God to handle. No matter how big that mask you have on, God can and will do exceedingly abundantly above all that we can ask for or even imagine.

We should not allow how it seems to determine the final outcome of our life; however, we should allow what is going on to be a stirring pot to break the cycle and say it's done with us. When we try to remove the mask by ourselves, it's going to be painful, frustrating, and rough. In the process of mask removal, people will try to remind us of why we can't become more than the obstacle we're facing. People will try to speak discouragement over our life, and it's up to us not to download or let those words plant seeds.

Chapter 3 — The Voice

In life, there are going to be different messages that will try to take root and plant a seed in your life. The question that we have to ask ourselves is, what seed will we allow, and what will we not allow? There are three voices that will have different messages and, depending on what we tell ourselves, will determine what voice we believe. The three voices are listed below:

The Voice Of The Impossible

There will be people in your life who will see what you go through and the genealogy of your family and will tell you that you can't do this and that because of who your family is and what you have encountered. They will tell you everything and try to make you believe it's impossible to achieve and do great things because of your circumstance.

They don't see that it's possible for you to elevate and grow because they have given the issues of life too much power and not believing that you're powerful to overcome and get through this life obstacle. There will be people who will use what you go through against you and do mockery of you because of the goals and dreams that you have set forth for yourself. And it's easy to allow what is happening around us to make us believe that it won't be possible, especially if

JOSIAS JEAN PIERRE

some of those messages are also coming from our own voice. The voice of the impossible is dangerous because it hinders you from growing. It hinders you from elevating to the next level and manifesting into the next chapter.

The impossible voice sees nothing but defeat, and it allows the setbacks to make the final decision of life when the setbacks are not the final decision of life. I can remember growing up, people could barely understand what I was saying because I was talking too fast. I wasn't talking fast on purpose; I didn't know how to annunciate my words so they could become clear when talking to others.

I had a stuttering issue. With that stuttering issue, people made fun of me because I have a clear disability. People will laugh at my dreams of being an author, speaker, and also someone of inspiration because they didn't believe I met the criteria. What they saw was limitations, and because of that, they limited what I could do because what was in the eye view didn't seem like it was going to be possible. What's in the eye view doesn't seem like it will flourish because of the setbacks. However, behind every setback, there's a bounce-back. When you have the voice of the impossible, it's going to be hard to see the bounce back happening in life. It's going to be hard to see yourself come out of the very thing you're going through because of limited thinking. And the seeds of destruction we have allowed ourselves or others to plant over our lives.

What are the impossible messages that we have listened to and adapted in our own life? Have you performed at a level where the fruits being reaped are good fruits? Or does your performance reflect fruits that are bad? We have to understand the voice of the impossible will blind us to see that there's a light at the end of the tunnel. The voice of the impossible will clog our minds to believe there's nothing better in store for us because of what we're facing.

I could have let the voice that others were trying to plant over my life take root, but I didn't because I was strongly convinced and believed that my purpose and mission in this life is to elevate, empower, and equip others with the tools they need to bounce back from their setbacks. Do not allow anyone to speak anything over your life that is not uplifting or encouraging because once it takes root, it will reap the seeds of destruction. Once it takes root, you will reap the seeds that later on you will regret. The second voice is listed below.

The Voice Of The Possible

There will be people in your life that will look at what you go through and will tell you, you can make it, you can overcome, you will bounce back, etc. They will speak life in the midst of your situation and believe that you will come out stronger, better, and wiser despite the storm of life. These people don't see what happens at the moment, but they see what happens at the moment can come out into something very good and powerful in the long haul.

The people who speak possibilities in the midst of what you're going through are the ones that will take along this fight for victory with you, but you first have to want it for yourself. When it comes to the voice of the possible, this is where people who don't have the voice of possibilities will feel like people are saying things to say things.

The reason why we have adopted the voice of the impossible for a long time is that when positivity and a message of hope come around, we feel like there's a catch behind the message of believing that you can, you must, and you will. We feel like that person wants something from us because they are using their voice as a voice of possibility. We have to want it for ourselves before anyone would want it for us. We have to be in the trenches for us before anyone else can be in the trenches right alongside us.

The question is, how badly do you want what you say you want? How motivated are you to get to those dreams and aspirations you may have set for yourself? What is your why behind why you do what you do? Those questions have to be answered with a possibility mentality. In order to have the possibility mentality, we first have to adapt to having the voice of the possible. The voice of the possible says, through it all, I am going to decree and declare there's hope in the midst of what I am in.

Through it all, I am going to speak those things as though they were; therefore, I am going to overcome this, I am going to bounce back from this, I will get through this, and this too shall pass. The voice of the possible does not let what is going on change the focus to the end goal. The voice of the possible does not let what's happening around them to determine the final outcome of their lives.

I have a mentor who has been my mentor since I was in middle school, and still, from that day, he and I have been very close. He's like a second father to me. My mentor would hear what I said and then would tell me to correct what I said. There were things that he would not allow me to speak about myself in his presence because he believed there was more in store, but I have to believe there's more in store for me. He was so focused on the possible, and even if he didn't know how it would look or turn out, he would never declare anything of the impossible. Since middle school, he would bring words of affirmation and will speak life over my life and keep on doing it despite how things looked in my life. There was a time when I asked him, Why do you believe in me so much? Why haven't you thrown the towel yet after you have seen where I am at in life?

He responded, *"I believe in you so much because you have potential, and you can and will do great things. As your mentor, I am going to do what I can to push you toward that very thing but quitting, and speaking words of destruction are not going to be an option. What do you want to be? Do you think you can get there by speaking what you're speaking over your life? Start speaking positivity, start speaking hope, and watch how you respond to the very things of life."*

I started speaking positivity, and I started speaking hope, and I started speaking those very things of what I wanted to become into the atmosphere. The more I kept on doing that, the more confidence arose. The mentality was different, and how I responded to the very things was different. I got into a habit of speaking positive affirmations over my life, and my message of positivity was still the same despite what I was facing.

The voice of the possible will open your mind to think differently in the midst of the response. It will open your eyes to see things differently and boost your confidence that you will get to the finish line. If you have people in your life who see value despite what you're going through, those are the type of people you want in your life. No matter how crushed, bruised, or in pain you are, your value of you will not change.

You can crush twenty dollars, step on it, and toss it into the trash; it still doesn't change the fact that the value is still twenty dollars. When you obtain the voice of the possible, you will not let what is happening around you or to you determine your value. The voice of the possible works wonders that the voice of the impossible can't do. The voice of the possible will lead you to things that people have said it's impossible for you to do. The third voice is listed below. This voice is the most important voice.

Your Voice

People can speak life over your life, and people can speak death over your life. Depending on what you speak about, you will determine what voice you will tend to believe. You're the foundation, and if the foundation is not rooted, everything else will not be stable. What you speak about you will determine how much drive you have, the mindset that you will carry, and the people you attract. A wise man once said, *"Show me your friends, and I will show you your future."* You're what you attract, and if you don't like what you're attracting into your circle, you have to change things around in your life. People can speak life and hope and fight the fight with you and will go above and beyond for you, but if you don't want it for yourself, what the other person is doing is not relevant.

What voice do you declare? What voice do you believe? Do you believe the voice of the impossibilities determines your final destination based on a setback? Or do you believe the voice of possibilities that says I will fight even though I am fighting alone because there's more to me than this situation that I am currently facing? The voice of possibilities says I was born on purpose, for a purpose, and with a purpose, and because of that, I have to be careful with what I decree and declare over my life.

Your voice is the powerful voice, and depending on what you declare over your life, it will determine which voice you will believe. If you don't have the voice of possibilities, start declaring positive affirmations over your life, and don't stop speaking those positive affirmations over your life.

When you can change your voice, you can change your world. When you can change your words, you can change your mindset. And when your mindset is changed, how you respond to things will change. When your mindset is changed, how you see things will change. The most powerful tool that we have as a being is the mindset we have. And if we don't protect our minds, we will be swayed to navigate toward the negative messages and not the positive messages.

It's easier to turn to the negative when negativity is the most common message that's being displayed in the world. It's easy to have the mindset of the impossible because we have been told by our peers, media, and family that certain things are impossible. When we look at the word impossible, it's not meant to be attached together. If we break down the word *impossible*, it really means I'm possible, or I am possible. Because of that, we have to have the voice of the possibilities and the voice of hope.

I believed so much that I could become an influencer, a speaker, an author, and an educator because of what I have seen in visions. When I believed that I could and switched my affirmations to positive affirmations, there was nothing in this world that could have made me believe the very thing won't be possible. I was rooted in the hope that I was hopeful even when it seemed like there was no hope around me. I was rooted in affirmations and believed with a mustard seed faith that I can, I will, and I must. I was so rooted in the possible that even when others told me it was not possible, I still stayed the course and ran my race as if I was almost to the finish line. I was so hungry to see the vision that I had seen at a young age play out in my life that I was willing to do anything and everything to make sure it manifested right in front of my eyes.

I had seen it before I have seen it and because of that, the grind made sense to keep on keeping on. I learned that if you have to see it to believe it, you will never see it. However, if you believe it before you see it, you will then see it. The motivation that I was getting made me believe I could do the very thing which people have deemed impossible over my life. Make sure the voice you're declaring and planting over your life is building you up and not tearing you apart.

Make sure the voice that you're speaking over your life is not the weapon that was formed against yourself. You are created for more, destined for more because you're more. You're more than enough, you're more than just a conqueror, and there's more in store for you that you have not seen or even touched. When we adapt the voice of possibilities, we can find ourselves stepping closer to the very thing which we may think we could never reach. Because I was so rooted in positive affirmations and believing the possible, there was a shift that took place that opened my eyes to the next level, which made me believe if these people can do it, I also can do it.

Chapter 4 — The Shift

In life, if we don't become sick and tired of being sick and tired, we will stay reaping what we say we want to see a change in our lives. However, when you are sick and tired of being sick and tired, you will do whatever you can to break the very thing that does not sit well within your spirit. At some point, we have to take some action and say *enough is enough*. Wanting a change but no action is just a wish.

You have to be that change agent and don't depend on anyone else to create a change you want to see manifest around you. I was tired of feeling what I was feeling and seeing what I was seeing. I wanted to see black people in areas outside of sports. I wanted to see black people outside of the mainstream media. Because I didn't see where black is besides in entertainment. I thought that would be the only thing out there for black people.

Since my dream was to become a motivational speaker, I wanted a platform where I could learn from someone who looked like me. But I wanted to see many people who look like me show me it's possible in the speaking arena. I wanted to be mentored and learn the ins and outs from someone who looks like me. There's nothing wrong with someone mentoring you who looks different from you. However, I knew if I had representation, the grind, and the determination would be different. During my senior year in high school, I saw and met different people who play major roles in the world to leave a greater impact on other people's lives. I went to a summit that was held on the college campus of Highline, located in Des-Moines, WA. This summit was called the *"Black and Brown Male Summit."*

This was not just a summit, but it was a life-changing event that took place where I saw people who look like me on platforms that I have dreamed of touching and reaching. I saw people who looked like me and who had similar life stories, which motivated me to keep on keeping on. I saw people who looked like me who had to go through things that were greater than my struggle. But because they overcame, it motivated me to believe I also would overcome what I was encountering and facing.

The first person that I met was John Carlos. John Carlos was the bronze-medal winner in the 200 meters at the 1968 Summer Olympics, where he displayed the Black Power salute on the podium with Tommie Smith. He was the speaker at the summit, which brought motivation to me. I left the summit empowered, equipped, and ready to face whatever obstacle may come my way because I have connected with influencers, impacters, and change-makers who poured into me. With the tools they gave me, I felt like I was ready to take on the battle. In the training that these black and brown speakers were giving, I left full, and I stayed full. Something happens when there's representation. When you see someone who looks like you are making it, you then have hope and encouragement that you, too, can make it. I went to the summit, which was the first year of this summit, and I did not know what to expect.

I came with a readiness to learn and soak every word that was being said either in the workshop or on the podium where the keynote speaker was speaking. One of the biggest things that the summit did was create space for students to talk about the very thing they are encountering or dealing with. I believe the summit was focused on the three E's — Evolving, Equipping, And Empowering.

Evolving young boys into young men, equipping them with the tools they need to overcome the obstacle they face, and empowering them to believe in themselves and stay on the course. Being in the summit equipped me to fight the good fight, empowered me to keep on keeping on and stay in the race no matter how difficult it could be, & evolved me to be the man I am today. This summit was a transformation summit and also a confirmation summit that I was where I needed to be. Before the summit was over, I told John Carlos that I would be a motivational speaker and that one day we might cross paths when I became an adult. Throughout the years, the summit increased, doubled, and tripled the number of attendees. In the first year of the summit, it was 12 to 15 young people. Year after year, the number increased to now the attendees are 400-500 black and brown youth.

The decision to come was the choice of the students to be present, active, and engaged. The summit took place on a Saturday from 08:00 to 04:00 pm. This was the first place where I saw representation in the education spectrum. Adults couldn't be where the students were, and students couldn't be where the adults were. The adults, & chaperones had their own section, and the youth had theirs.

The reason why it happened the way it happened was that the summit wanted to lift the voice of the black and brown youth. Be you, be authentic, be real, and don't be afraid to speak about difficult topics. Because of that, we were able to break the strongholds and attack the barriers that we were maybe facing as black and brown youth. We were able to share our own voices and talk about the very thing that is impacting us on a daily basis. Vulnerability happened in the space, tears were shed in the space, the transformation was taking place in the space, and healing was taking place in the space. When I saw there were those who looked like me in different aspects of life outside of sports, and they encountered difficulties getting to where they are at, I didn't have any excuse.

My excuses were gone, but the fire in me started to burn. I was so inspired by the workshops and the speakers that it motivated me to press the gas on my goals and visions and let go of excuses. The moment where I did that, I was clearing off the goals that I had written down. Opportunities were coming my way that I didn't look for, but they just came to my table, which I couldn't reject.

At 17, I was the keynote speaker for the 20th anniversary of the City of SeaTac. A city located in WA state. At 17, I was one of four youth speakers presenting at the national ASHA (American School Health Association) conference in Kansas City, MO. I was talking in front of hundreds of educators, lawyers, & doctors, bringing a message that would shift their seats and shift their thought processes. I was talking about the importance of representation and also the disparities in every system in America but mainly the education system. When those two opportunities came to my doorstep, all I could say was, Thank you, God, for putting me in the black and brown male summit in such a time like this. I had to go back and give credit to the summit because the summit did wonders for me, and I would be remiss if I didn't give credit to whom credit is due. This summit woke me up to take my goals more seriously. It woke me up to do what I needed to complete what I said I wanted to see complete in my life. I didn't know when or how it was going to be done; however, I knew if I just kept on going, then eventually, I would reap that seed.

I felt like I was undefeated because my mentality was an undefeated mentality. My mentality was a bounce-back champion mentality. No matter what was coming my way, I believed I would conquer, defeat, and destroy that obstacle. This summit was the turning point in my life. It turned around for the good because that's when true hope started rising for me.

It turned around for the better because that's when I felt like I was one step closer to achieving that dream as an author and a speaker. Because of the impact that the summit had left on my life in high school, I started coming back year after year to help out and assist in whatever way I could. I came back to be a part of the solution of impact for the greater good.

I took on a role at the college once I graduated high school as Student Ambassador. I was giving tours around the college campus, traveling throughout different counties, sharing my story with the youth, and also being a part of the college fairs that were taking place. My position was in the outreach department, so anything outreach-related, I was a part of. I helped assist with the summit and made myself available for whatever needed to be done because I wanted others to have the experience that I had. I graduated from the college in 2013; therefore, I wasn't working there any longer; however, I was still a part of the summit. This time, I was coming to the summit as a workshop presenter and a facilitator. Now we are ten years into this summit, and I have attended it every single year.

After graduating, year after year from there, I was presenting and bringing a message to the youth that they will leave equipped, empowered, and evolved. Equipped to face the giants in their lives, empowered to not give up when it's difficult, and evolve into a better version of themselves. This time, I am sharing the platform with John Carlos. The picture on the left was him and I when he spoke at the 1st black and brown male summit when I was in high school. The picture on the right is him, and I know this time that I am an adult, and we both speak at the black and brown male summit. I did a workshop presentation, and John Carlos and I shared the platform bringing a message to the youth. When we both saw each other, we were in awe and just smiling so big because he remembered the person I was when I was in high school. He remembered the impact that he had left on my life before the event was over. He also remembered that I told him that I would become a motivational speaker and one day share the stage together being an adult.

And it happened. We hugged and just laughed together, and I kept him updated about what had taken place in my life. The very place that impacted my life and changed my focus all the way around is the very place where I was able to share the platform with the great icon John Carlos. The same place that gave me a shift of life and restored a lot of things in my life that needed to be restored is where I was able to come as an adult and bring a message with one of the greatest who has done it.

What are some things in your life where you're sick and tired of being sick and tired? With that thing that is making you sick and tired of being sick and tired, what shift are you needing? What is it that you want to see in order for you to take action? It's not about what happens, but it's about how you respond to the very thing that is happening.

It's not our fault that we were born in the situations we were born in, the conditions we are born in, but it is our fault if we choose to repeat it. It is our fault if we choose to carry it forward. It is our fault if we accept it as is and do not do something about it. It is our fault if we tend to become silent about the thing that is bringing damage.

I knew I needed a summit that was only for black and brown individuals. I knew I needed a summit where representation mattered and my voice and cry were heard. It took a summit for me to speak at a national conference, be the keynote for the city's anniversary, and be the keynote at the legislation conference in Olympia, WA. It took a summit for me to hit the ground strongly, and I never turned back because of the amount of representation that was there at the summit. It is up to us to draw the line on the ground and say it's no more. I can't let this continue; I can't let this manifest after me, I have to do something different, so I can leave something different. I have to draw a line in the sand and say, today is the day that I will no longer....

Today is the day that I will not continue to do or have.... Today is the day that I will not.... Today is the day when I am going to... Whatever it is, you have to draw the line and declare differently and do differently. If we know what it tastes like, why choose to repeat it? If we know what the pain feels like, why choose to repeat it? If we knew we didn't like the taste, why would we be okay with carrying that taste down to someone else? You have to be serious about what you want to see manifest and grow because nobody else can't be serious about you. If that means cutting folks from your life so you can have a shift, then you have to cut folks in your life. If that means you have to stop entertaining what you have always entertained, then you have to stop doing that entertaining. If you know the shift that you want to see is going to require you to cancel some people out of your life, would you be okay with that? If you know the shift is going to require you not to go places that you used to go to, would you be okay with that? I ask these questions because there are times we want to see a shift happen, but we want to stay at a neutral level where we can still do what we want to do and how we want to do it.

When you're expecting a shift in life, it's going to require you to let go of things and people just so you can elevate and blossom to the next level. In order for you to start the new stages, the old things must go because not everything can go with you to the next level. The stuff that does not have value must go because you need things that will bring value.

If it's not bearing positive fruits, then it's not worth keeping. How hungry are you to see a shift in your life? What are you willing to do to see that shift manifest? If it means being alone during the season of the shift, would you be okay with that? If not, why? There's a story of two twin boys who had a father who was a drunkard. One of the boys was a heavy drinker, and the other boy didn't drink. The question was asked to the twins, why do you drink, and why do you not? The twin who drinks said, *"I drink because I see my dad do it."* The other twin said, *"I don't drink because I have seen my dad do it."* At the moment, it didn't make sense, but after further processing it, it made clear sense. In life, you have options, and you decide what it is that you want to do and how you want to do it. Two identical twin boys who grew up together witnessed the same thing of their father being drunker but made two different decisions on how to move forward in their lives.

The twin who didn't drink has seen the impact that drinking had caused his father and the damage in the marriage, and how much toll it took on the family. Because of what he has seen, he said, this is not going to be me. I am not going to do that. I have to shift this for my family; therefore, this won't be something that will be carried.

The boy had seen the pain from seeing his family fall apart, and he didn't want that to be carried on when he had kids in the future. He said the reason why he didn't drink was that he didn't like the pain that he felt and did not want to carry it over to his own children. He was willing to risk it all just so a shift could happen in his family. He was willing to do whatever he could just so this experience couldn't be passed down to his legacy.

Many people didn't understand why this twin boy was not like the others in his family who were drinkers and partiers, and they assumed maybe he thought he was too cool to do the family things. When in actuality, he didn't want to be around what hurt him and what was bringing him pain, and all he hoped and wanted was a shift to happen so the family could be together again. The other twin boy who did drink said he drank because his father did it. The other twin boy followed in his dad's footsteps because he wanted to do whatever his dad did despite the pain and the hurt that was caused.

Despite whatever he could be feeling, he admired his father so much that he felt it was worth going through the pain just to be like his daddy. He felt like he was a part of the family because everyone else in the family was doing it. He wanted to be included no matter what, and the other twin wanted to be excluded from what was bringing him pain and the family pain that the family refused to acknowledge.

The family uses alcohol to be silent about the pain, while the twin boy, who doesn't drink, depends on his circle to help him navigate through this hurt and hopes a shift will manifest. It wasn't until the father was diagnosed with alcohol poisoning and was told by doctors that there was too much damage to the kidney and might need a new kidney.

The doctors went on and told the family, *"If nobody does stop this cycle, your seeds can be affected by this very disease because it's in you. Someone in this family must take a stand and say not anymore."* The twin brother, who was drinking, told the doctors, *"Everybody in my family drinks except my twin brother. This was normal for us, and plus I wanted to be like my dad, so I did whatever my daddy did. My uncle, my grandparents, my aunts, and my sisters all drink except my twin. However, I do not want to have alcohol poisoning or be in the state that my father is in. I will rise up to the task and break this for my family that I have right now, and It will not be carried on. It will be done with me, and my seeds don't have to face this."*

The twin who doesn't drink told his brother and his family, *"I didn't have to drink to know how painful this is. It's sad that you all try to use alcohol to have a shift that is leading to death, but I am using my peers who are standing in the gap with me to fight this obstacle just so we can have a shift and live. I was tired of seeing how dad was violent every time he came home; I was tired of seeing how mom would go hide when dad would be tipsy or even drunk. I was tired of everything, and because of this tiredness, I chose to be alone while you all drank as if that was going to change the real issue. I didn't drink and won't ever drink because I don't want to repeat a cycle that should never be repeated to begin with. It's sad that dad has to be in this state for you all to see the big damage that I have been speaking about for a long time. It's sad that it took a doctor to tell us dad needs a new kidney due to the alcohol just for us to wake up. What now? What do you all have to say now? While you all thought I was crazy fighting for a healthy space and a healthy environment, now dad is here in this position. Don't tell the doctor or me what you're going to do or think about doing. If you want different, you will do differently. Let your actions show that you're done. And if this does not make you long for a shift, then I don't know what will."* The twin brother and the rest of the family went home and looked at every alcohol bottle and case, threw it all in the trash, and said not anymore, we need a shift, and the shift is going to happen today.

I share this story because, in life, there might be people fighting for a shift because the pain they have encountered from the act is drawing them away from being a part of the transaction. There will be people around us who will look at you differently because you're not a part of the masses. People will make fun of you because you stand to fight. Don't let what others say or change your focus on the shift you want to see manifest. You know how the feeling tastes like, and it's up to you to determine if you want that taste to be passed down to those coming after you. Sometimes it will take something happening close to us to make a decision that enough is enough. It will take something close to us to say I am done; no more of this and that is happening. Sometimes it will take what's dearest to our hearts to draw a line in the sand and start waking up to what was there the whole time.

I remember when my mother was diagnosed with breast cancer in 2019. It was four months after my brother and I bought our property. Three words you don't ever want to hear in the same sentence, *"I have cancer."*

Every part of me broke and torn apart. Every piece of me didn't know what to do. I was going to work with tears consistently flowing down my eyes. I was going to church with tears flowing down my eyes. I didn't know what to do or how to process it. Around this season, I was already getting spiritually weak, and I knew what I needed to do to get rejuvenated spiritually, but I always slacked or didn't even give it any thought.

It took the diagnosis of cancer for me to take action for my spiritual growth. It took the action of cancer for me to press in prayer and fight for victory. It took the action of cancer and seeing my mom fighting this disease for me to activate and release everything within me. I had a fight in me that I never knew I had in me. I had to call on people to fight this fight with me. Months later, the doctors told my mom, *"You're cancer free."*

Behind this cancer, the relationship between my mom and her sister increased. Something horrific had to take place just so I take action in my spiritual growth and the relationship between family could be reconnected again. Today, my mother and her sister have one of the strongest relationships that they have ever had. Today, my spiritual walk has been one of the strongest walks I have ever had. It took cancer to break things in my life and be put back together again to strengthen spiritually. It took a life event for me to see where I was spiritually.

It took me almost losing my mother for me to do a spiritual evaluation and a spiritual check and ensure I never get to the level where I was spiritually. What are some things in your life you know you need to take action on, but you're being stagnant? What are some things in your life you know need attention but you're just ignoring it? What are some things in your life where you know what to do but do not choose to do it because of priorities that are not in order? In this shift, I realized that God would use what is close to us to get our attention.

He will use what's dearest to us to wake us up. Whatever you want to see change, take action to bring that change forward. Fight the good fight, and don't wait until something has to happen in order for us to wake up. If nobody is joining the fight with you, keep on fighting. If nobody is standing with you, keep on standing. If nobody is running the course with you, keep on running because it will all pay out in the end.

If you want to see that shift, it's going to require you to shift the belief you have about yourself. If you want to see a shift in your life, it's going to require you to change how you speak about yourself. It's going to require you to change that radio station that plays over and over again.

The question that must be pondered is, are you ready for the shift? Are you ready to break barriers so you can become the best you possible? Are you ready to become an obstacle breaker for you and your legacy? Are you ready to wake up? Not wake up from your sleep but wake up from the number of excuses you have told yourself just so a shift can manifest in your life. You have to be so hungry for a shift to the point when negativity comes your way that you let that become your fuel to keep on running the race.

Chapter 5 — 2020 Wake Up

Twenty-twenty was known as the year of vision. COVID-19 led into 2020, which was a year where a lot of people had woken up. This was the year known as the vision year. People were waking up and seeing things in a different way. I have always said that if 2020 didn't bring out the hunger and motivation in you, nothing will. There were a lot of setbacks in 2020, which showed many of us where we are and what we need to do.

It also showed us where we are, but we still chose to make excuses for it. This was my 27th chapter, and I didn't know what was happening in this chapter, but one thing I saw was the true focus of the church. I have seen how the church was preaching an agenda that was not God's agenda. The church said, "Thus says the Lord," and God didn't say one thing about what these false prophets were saying out of their mouth.

We have seen the church use the podium and water down the message to bring a feeling-good message but not a message that will bring conviction. The church was more interested in having butts in seats instead of souls in seats because they cared more about having more bucks. More butts equal more bucks. And if the church can just keep on preaching a feeling-good message and a message that will be an itching message to hear, then the butts will still fill seats. Timothy 4 1-2 gives a charge and an active call of what needs to be done. It says in Timothy 4:2, *"Preach the word; be prepared in season, and out of season; correct, rebuke, and encourage — with great patience and instructions."* This is what the preachers need to bring a message that will bring conviction and not water down the gospel.

However, we see verse three of Timothy come into full effect, where people have boxed God into their political party as if God was affiliated with a political agenda. Let's not forget the parties were man-made, and God is not included in any of those parties. Also, let's not forget this nation is a godless nation. They will confess to God with their lips, but their heart is far from God.

In verses 3-4 of Timothy, it says, *"For the time will come when people will not put up with sound doctrine. Instead, to suit their own desires, they will gather around them a great number of teachers to say what their itching ears want to hear. They will turn their ears away from the truth and turn aside to myths."* I truly believe that we have seen the verses of 3-4 play out in the year 2020. It had been played out for a long time, but this year was a wake-up year where we had no choice but to see how distant the church is from God. We had no choice but to see how man's agenda was being played out, which was deemed God's agenda. We had no choice but to see the lack of love provided that year. Twenty-twenty wasn't only the year of civil unrest but also the year of elections. One thing we have seen the church has done was false prophesy, saying God said this when he never said it. This is why scripture says we have to *"Test the spirit by the spirit"* because if it can't be lined up with the word of God, then it's not God.

If you can't find a reference point of scripture to match what the prophesy is, then it was not God. A prophecy is a confirmation of what God has already said. One thing the bible didn't say is that God is a republican or a democrat. The word of God does not say that; however, it does say that the government will be on his shoulders. God doesn't need a political party to do what he wants to do because he is God, and he doesn't need us; we need him.

Too often, we view this walk with God as if we are doing him a service, as if, if you don't want to be used, God can't move. God will move with or without us. His plan and will will move with or without us. This was the year when the church got exposed, and the heart of the church showed so much that people had left the church because of man's agenda and not God's agenda. People have been so swayed into the false prophets' messages that they don't even tend to open scripture for themselves to see what scripture has said because what the person was saying on the podium sounds good because that's what they wanted to hear. The pain of others was being silent, and the talk of justice was being ignored because preachers didn't want to offend anyone. Preachers didn't want to push away those if they preached about justice & equality. Maybe the folks who give lots of tithes and offerings will stop coming to the church. I have seen churches silent the talk about injustice and have said, let's not talk about it because it's not God.

However, the scripture says in Proverbs 28:5, *"Evil men do not understand justice, But those who seek the Lord understand all."* When I read that scripture, I asked myself, does the church really understand who God is? God is a God of justice, and if we say we love God, we must stand for Justice and speak out against injustice. We have a duty as believers to stand for truth even if nobody doesn't want to stand with us. We have a demand to be unapologetic about what we believe in because, at the end of the day, it's not for the man that we live; it's for Christ that we live. And if folks want to leave the church because the word brings conviction, then let them leave. If folks want to leave the church because you're preaching Bible, let them leave.

If folks want to get mad at you because you're preaching about a topic that is uncomfortable to talk about, let them get mad. The word of God is not easy to digest, but it needs to be digested. Hebrews 4:12 says, *"For the word of God is alive and active. Sharper than any double-edged sword, it penetrates even to dividing soul and spirit, joints and marrow; it judges the thoughts and attitudes of the heart (New International Version)."*

If the message is going forth and it does not bring any sort of conviction to the body, then are we really saved? Since the word of God is alive and active, and it's sharper than any double-edged sword, why are we scared if it makes someone bleed? I ask these questions because, in 2020, we saw the opposite taking place in the church.

The talk around justice was not talked about, false prophets were falsely testifying, and the heart of the church was exposed in many different ways. How so? One of the biggest things that we have seen was the back-to-back incidents of what was taking place in the hands of law enforcement but also the silence of the church. We have seen Ahmaud Arbery, Breonna Taylor, George Floyd, and Manuel Ellis, to name a few of the people who lost their lives in 2020. Because of this, there was a protest of "Black Lives Matter" taking place throughout the nation.

As someone who has been at the forefront for justice even in the rally, I have seen how the church will try to silence the pain of black people and say, *"It's not of God that people are taking the streets. It's not of God to fight and stand for Justice. It's not of God to do X, Y & Z."* I could remember sitting there being furious because the God in the Bible is not the God these church leaders were talking about. The God in the Bible is a God of justice, and he stands for Justice and speaks out against injustice.

The God in the Bible stands for the oppressed and etc. When I heard what the church was saying and talking about, I had to really put it in check real quick. I had to realize because the pain is not on their doorstep, they don't think it's real. Because they will never have to encounter what it is that many people of color have to encounter, they don't think it's real.

We were forced to watch back-to-back incidents of injustice taking place on national television, and if you still don't understand the why behind the fight, then you are a part of the problem. I have heard how people will say the BLM group is doing this and that in the rally, but they are not even at the rally to really see what is going on. People believe the news when the news isn't present from the beginning to the end. As someone who was there on the front lines taking these streets while we were unarmed, chanting, crying, and wanting answers, I know the violence that took place in the city did not happen by the black people. However, because it happened at a BLM rally, black people were getting blamed for the violence that was taking place in the city, and it was not the black people. According to the *Armed Conflict Location &*

Event Data Project (ACLED), more than 93% of the protest has been peaceful.

ACLED is funded by the State Department's Bureau of Conflict and Stabilization Operations as well as foreign governments and other organizations, including the Dutch Ministry of Foreign Affairs, the German Federal Foreign Office, the Tableau Foundation, the International Organization for Migration, and The University of Texas at Austin.

They rely on data collected from the U.S. Crisis Monitor, which is a joint project led by ACLED and Princeton University's Bridging Divides Initiative — that tracks and publishes real-time data on political violence and demonstrations in the U.S. in order to "Establish an evidence base from which to identify risks, hotspots, and available resources to empower local communities in times of crisis."[1]

For years I have been on the front lines leading the march or even doing security for the march. For years I've been at the forefront, asking for justice, and what the media portrays is not what is happening on the front lines. I could tell you stories about how police will show up to where the protest is happening, and

---

[1] 93% of Black Lives Matter Protests Have Been Peaceful, New Report Finds. (2020, September 5). Time. https://time.com/5886348/report-peaceful-protests/

hours beforehand, they are destroying property, and the BLM is getting blamed for it.

I can tell you how the cars were blowing up in Seattle and how the police department played a role in the blowing up of the cars. I can tell you how youth/kids with their hands up asking cops questions are being shot with tear gassed as if it was illegal to ask cops questions. The worst part, the cops didn't get in trouble for it, they kept their job, and some even got a promotion after the transaction. I can tell you how the police departments had a game plan to do what they wanted to do, but then the folks at the rally would get the blame for the transaction the cops were doing.

If you're not at the march, you would just believe the news; however, 99% of the people who are there can tell you something different than what the media is telling the people. I went to the forefront to be real eyewitness, not only as an activist but also to give the facts to those who weren't there physically to see what was really going on. I remember when the cars blew up in Seattle. I went on Facebook live, telling people what was really going on and what was happening in Seattle before they got bombarded with wrong information from the news. People were running left and right while we heard shots fired left and right. Every time a car blew up, here's SPD (Seattle Police Department) boom, boom, boom,

boom, & boom. Shooting tear gassed. Here's my question.

There are hundreds of cops near their own vehicles; how did you allow someone to get that close to your vehicle and put it on fire, and nobody didn't arrest that person on the spot? The person who caused the crime was a White woman named Margaret Channon, who was arrested nearly two weeks after she was caught on video using fire and aerosol cans to light police vehicles on fire. [1]

Why did it take this long for them to catch the suspect when cops sat there and watched it happen? Every time this woman blew up a police car, the officers shot tear gas at the peaceful protestors as if we had a role to play in the car blowing up that the police department saw with their two eyes who did the transaction but took no action for arrest. I told the folks at the church these incidents that happened Live, and it was justified as if it was okay if people who are White could do these transactions in the name of black lives matter. It was justified as if their reasoning for doing the act was valid, but having a march for Black Lives Matter was not valid. I started looking at church leaders differently. I looked at church leaders differently, but I didn't look at God differently because I know who God is, and I know him for myself; therefore, there's nothing a person can do to make me believe differently about God.

I started to think about the history of how Black churches and Black homes were vandalized, torches were thrown at the property, etc., and everyone was silent. I started to think about the statement of all lives matter and how ignorant a statement that is especially knowing systematically that Black Lives Never Mattered in America. I found myself over and over again explaining to people the tears that black folks cry, but it keeps falling on deaf ears.

I have looked throughout history and realized that we didn't move much; it's just the same struggle but a different generation. It's the same issue, but it just looks different. But is it really different? I look at the original writings of the pledge of allegiance and ask questions about why the original context was changed. I don't even think many people know that the pledge of allegiance has changed. The pledge of allegiance was written in August 1892 by a socialist minister Francis Bellamy. The original form of the pledge of allegiance reads, "*I pledge allegiance to my Flag and the Republic for which it stands, one nation, indivisible, with liberty and justice for all.*" (ushistory.org)

It's very important that we look at the original pledge of allegiance, and some key components of the original form tell us what the system represents. When we look at the word "*my*" in the pledge of allegiance, we have to view the color of the flag. The flag colors are red, white, and blue. When the writer says *"my flag,"* who is mine? Does *"my flag"* also represent the black folks who fought for this country no matter the era and still get treated poorly? Does it represent the black people who fought for this country, but the country doesn't want anything to do with their existence? Does it represent the people of color who walk in this life and has to fight against a system that wants to see them fail instead of succeeding? The second thing we have to notice in the original context of the pledge of allegiance is that God was never mentioned. We keep hearing how this nation is a God nation, and truly, this nation is a godless nation. The fruit that this nation bear represents that it's a godless nation. The actions that have been done over and over again show it's a godless nation. I have heard church people say if the pastor preaches about justice, they are leaving the congregation. I have heard people in the church bluntly say in front of my face, *"I don't believe Black Lives Matter; I believe All Lives Matter."* If you don't believe black lives matter, what do you call a black life? How can you say you believe all lives matter, but you don't believe that black lives matter? That was one of the biggest things that irritated me because then I couldn't really spend time with you any longer. I can't even call you a friend because I know how you stand and where you stand when it comes to those who look like me. I know your position, and because of that, I have to cancel the relationship I had with you.

2020 gave me a different awakening which led me to take a sabbatical. This fight for equality and justice is not an easy fight; however, it's a fight that must continue. When you see how the heart of supposedly God's people showed in 2020, I had to take a few steps back. I took a few steps back because the heart of God was not shown whatsoever. There wasn't any compassion for those who were impacted by the injustices going on in the world. The church was silent, and being silent about what matters is very dangerous. It's in difficult times when you see the heart get exposed, and I truly believe that 2020 was the year where the heart of the church was exposed. Because of this exposure, many people walked away from the four walls of the building. I say building because it's a building. Don't get the church mistaken for a building because the church is the people, not the building. The building is a place where we gather to worship, but the building is not the church. When I looked into the 21st-century church, I realized how much of a polluted gospel is being preached. I realize that we are so afraid of being held responsible that we limit what we preach as if we don't have a demand to preach the truth and nothing but the truth. If we say we believe in the book, we must believe in the whole book and not just be a part of the book.

We can't pick and choose what we should or shouldn't preach because of the feelings of the congregation. If it's in the word, it needs to be preached, and just because some may not like it, it does not mean that it shouldn't be preached. 2020 was a civil unrest year throughout the nation, and it was also the year where we saw nationwide how the church turned a blind eye to be a light in a time like this. It was also the year when the church refused to be the light but instead chose to be silent at a time when our presence could have made a difference. When I say Black lives matter, I am not referring to no organization; I am referring to the black lives you see every day. Don't get black life mistaken for an organization because when the statement is being said, the organization is not being thought of. Publicly, I don't support or stand for the organization, but I do stand and support the statement black lives matter which led me to fight the good fight so black lives can matter systematically. Because of my fight and my stands, people in the building started looking at me differently and pushing me away slowly because I was very vocal about the very thing the church was silent about.

Some have called me a radical because I was unapologetic about my stands and what I had to say. Some have told me that I need to be less vocal about what I am saying out loud because it's offending too many people, and that's not good. Well, if the truth offends, let it offend. If what I say is bringing a conviction, then let it convict. If you say you're a believer and you don't have a conviction, then you need to question your salvation.

I have seen the church care more about people feeling instead of standing for the truth to the point where the message will get watered down just so it won't offend anyone. The 21st-century church has been so consumed with a watered-down gospel that people can't even tell the difference because our reflection looks just like theirs. If the pain and hurt of your neighbor don't affect you, do you really have a heart of God? Even if you don't understand what they are going through but the fact that they are hurting and we choose to turn a blind eye instead of bringing assistance, what does that say about who we believe in? We have to understand through us, people will see Christ not because of what we confess but because of the fruits that we manifest.

And if we don't have any fruits that Christ bares, do we really believe in Christ? In the book of Matthew, chapter 25:31-40, we see that Christ is separating the sheep and the goats. He puts the sheep on his right and the goats on his left. Christ starts telling the sheep to come and take the inheritance; the kingdom has prepared for them since the creation of the world.

Christ went on and said in 25:35-36, "*For I was hungry, and you gave me something to eat, I was thirsty, and you gave me something to drink, I was a stranger, and you invited me in, I needed clothes, and you clothed me, I was sick, and you looked after me, I was in prison, and you came and visited me."* From there, we see in 25:37 that the righteous started asking questions to figure out when they did all this. Christ replied in 25:40, saying, *"Whatever you did for one of the least of these brothers and sisters of mine, you did for me."* (New International Version)

There is nothing in the Bible that would suggest that it is possible to separate love for God from love for people. When the church becomes silent about what matters and turns a blind eye to those who are hurting and wounded, we are also doing it unto God. The ministry of being present speaks more volumes than anything else. In 25:41 of Matthew, we see Christ telling the goats to depart away from him because when he was hungry, thirsty, a stranger, needing clothes, sick, and in prison, they weren't there to be present.

The goat then asked, when did we see you naked, hungry, thirsty, sick, or in prison and did not help you? The Lord replied, *"Whatever you did not do for one of the least of these, you did not do for me."* Being present can be one of the best presents anyone could ever have because it can go a long way. Being present can change a life beyond measure.

I saw in 2020 how much the church had pushed those away who were hurting and wounded instead of bringing them in and being present at a time when people needed it the most. I have seen how the church has silenced the cries of the broken instead of choosing to be a light in the moment. I have seen discussions get ignored because the body of believers may not be ready to face reality even though it's in the word. Whatever you do unto the least of them, you have also done it unto God. When the church refuses to be present and stand for justice and speak out against injustice, it's as if we are validating the injustices taking place since we are turning a blind eye to the situation. As the church, we have to be unapologetic about our faith so that we will not waive our stands or distort the message of God because of the feelings of the people. First and foremost, God is not affiliated with any political agenda, and when we attach God to a political party, what you're saying is that God is limited. What we are doing is putting God in a box when he is too big to be put in a box.

Isaiah 55:8-9 says, *"For my thoughts are not your thoughts, neither are your ways are my ways, declares the LORD. As the heavens are higher than the earth, so are my ways higher than your ways and my thoughts than your thoughts."* We have been so indoctrinated into a political party we automatically stay where we are and look at things in the view of the political lens, then call it God's lens. In reality, there's not one lens of humankind that can be compared to the lens that God has. We need to have the lens of God and not the other way around. Because of the incidents that happened in my life and even the year 2020, I didn't know until later that it was launching me into the next chapter. Not just the work for activism but also the work of transformation and changing lives for the better. I started seeing my pain turn into purpose. I started seeing how I was being extended and launched for the work of impact, not realizing how many lives were touched in the process. I started seeing Romans 8:28, *"And we know that all things God works for the good of those who love him, who have been called according to his purpose."* Come in full effect. I have seen many times how things turned around for good, but for some reason, It wasn't clear that it was for the better good. What the devil meant for evil, God can turn around for good. I have seen and noticed how God used the storms, the fight for justice for good. Through it, all my pain was turning into purpose.

Chapter 6 — Turning Your Pain Into Purpose

One of the biggest questions that people always ask is why? What was the purpose behind all this? Why am I facing this? Is there even light at the end of the tunnel? These are common questions we have when we are going through the storms of life that we are in. The storms of life have one purpose, which is to push us into our purpose.

The trials and tribulations we are in are there to do one thing, push us into purpose. I know we heard it's not about what we go through, but it's about how we respond to what we are going through. The pain that I have endured throughout all these years has motivated me and positioned me to step into my purpose.

When going through the trials and storms, it didn't feel good, nor did it make sense, but looking back at how many people have been inspired and motivated to keep on keeping on because of my story has changed my focus to look at the trials and tribulations as worth it. Through it all, I have seen how God was with me every step of the way. God had to do a work in me before he could do the work through me. I was looking for God to do the outer work but neglected the inner work. I didn't realize at the moment that whatever was on the inside would show up on the outside; therefore, the inside needed cleaning and work to be done before the work could be done. What is the inside of you that you're holding onto that you refuse to let go of? Many of us have things in our past that we are holding onto, and we ask God to do what he needs to do in our lives; however, the very thing we are holding onto is the very thing God is trying to release, but we don't want to release it.

What if the very thing that we are holding onto is the very thing that is holding us back from elevating and growing into our purpose? The test of life comes from God, and if you're on the test, it's because he knows you will get through it. We have to grow through what we go through just so someone else can have an impact and receive a massive breakthrough.

The trials and tribulations of life have one job to position us toward what God has in store for us. The problem is that we are trying to be god and get mad at God when we are in the way of what he needs to do the way he needs to do it. Instead of us waiting for God to show up, we would rather go back to the very thing that will make us feel good at the moment but have a negative impact in the long run. We have become so consumed with wanting it right now that patience has been viewed as an insult. We don't even want to go through the process anymore because we don't want to wait for the outcome; we want it instant. We treat God like it's an ATM where we only access it when it's needed. But if it's not needed, we won't even go to him. God is not an ATM and should not be treated as such. When we talk about turning our pain into purpose, we have to understand the identity that we are connected with in Christ Jesus.

We have to understand that in the hands of God, he has our lives mapped out from the beginning and to the and we have to trust in his master plan and know that we are in good hands. I was always eager to get through the fruits but not plant no seeds. I was eager to reap what I wanted to see but did not trust the process to plant the seed that I wanted to reap.

It wasn't until when I became very tired of trying to figure this out by myself, I made a decision to deny myself and pick up the cross and follow him. I said God, you have the master plan, and you know more about me than I know about myself; therefore, I am picking up your cross and trusting that you will do what you said you would do. I am trusting that you will manifest what you say you will manifest. I am going to put my life in you and believe that you will do exceedingly abundantly above all that I can ask for or even imagine. God, whatever you want to do in this season, please don't do it without me. I want to be a part of whatever you're doing in any season. I want to be a part of the season of healing, the season of breakthrough, the season of restoration, etc. Whatever it is, God, don't do it without me. I came to

God broken and giving everything that I have, fully surrendering to him so he can use me in a way where he will get the glory and not me.

I wanted God to use me and have all the credit and honor be pointed right back to him because I can't boast nor take credit for what he is going to do in my life. The more I chased after him, the more the fire in me was stirring up to do the work that he had assigned me to do. Every step of the way, God was there. In order for me to understand how the pain of life can turn into purpose, I had to believe that there was a purpose in the midst of pain.

I had to believe that this was not the final chapter of my life, and if I was still breathing, it was because my work was not done here yet. I want to let you know that if you're still breathing, it's because there's still more work in you, and God is not done with you yet. I want to let you know that for every part of the mess of life, God can use that as a message; for every test of life, God can use that as a testimony; and for every misery of life, God can use that as a ministry. God can use what we thought was purposeless to show us how it was purposeful. God can use what we thought could not be worth it and show us how every bit of it was worth it. God can use what we have deemed impossible and shows us through it all that it's possible. We have to know and fully understand what is impossible for man; it's possible for God. I understand you might be at your breaking point, and you're just done and tired and want to quit because what you are facing feels like it's too heavy.

I understand you want answers right now, and you don't want to wait any longer because it's getting too much to handle. I want you to understand, in the midst of your breaking point, to go ahead and surrender and give it to God because he will restore what you thought could never be restored. I want you to go ahead and just release that burden to him because it's not our duty to carry our burden. God will take care of that burden that we have. I am not telling you about what I heard; I am telling you from experience. I truly believe their multiple ways in which your pain can turn into purpose. But I truly believe these five steps can help you to turn your pain into purpose. These items are listed below:

Knowing It's Not A Mistake

So many times, when we go through trials and tribulations of life, we think of the worst and dwell on the worst. We have to know when the forks hit the road in life; it's only there to better you and not destroy you. It might feel like destruction is happening, but the old things must fall so the new things can come.

When we talk about turning your pain into purposive, we have to understand that it's not a mistake that you face what you face. I had to understand that I was not an accident and I was here for a purpose, with a purpose, and on purpose. I had to change my thought process to know that it was positioning me for something greater that I can't see right now.

It's just positioning me for a greater impact and for a greater message that can change the lives of thousands throughout the nation. I want you to know and fully understand that nothing about you is an accident, and nothing about the placement of your family is an accident; you're there for a purpose, on purpose, and with a purpose. The trials of life that are happening to you are just creating a message for those who are connected to you so you can show them if you can do it, they can do it. What you go through is not for you, but it's for someone else out there who needs to hear how you made it through. What you go through is just preparing you to step into levels where your light can shine upon many and give hope to so many people.

I remember in 2006 when God delivered me from epilepsy after suffering from that for the first 13 years of my life; he birthed a passion in me for folks with disabilities and those that have an IEP (Individual Education Plan). Today I speak in front of schools, organizations, and colleges to address learning differences, especially when it comes to those with disabilities: Seeable disability or non-seeable disability. Today I speak in front of kids, youth, young adults, and adults who have a disability and inspire them to stay on the course even if it feels like it's hard to stay within the course.

What the devil meant for evil, God turned around for good. I could've dwelled on what was happening in the present moment and missed the purpose of impact, which will take place right after. A lot of times, we won't know our passion in life until we go through things in life that will turn into passion. We won't know what we are commissioned to do until we go through some storms and make it out of some storms to see what is birthing inside of each and every one of us. The second thing that we must do to turn our pain into purpose is listed below.

Fully Surrendering

We have to know and fully understand that this life is not meant to walk alone and that we have God who will walk this journey with us. We have to come to the point of fully surrendering to God and say, God, I am surrendering to your will and to your ways, and I am tired, God, of going through life by myself. What is it that you have for me? What is it that you commissioned me to do? In life, we have come to a point where we feel like we have to go through life by ourselves.

The media has a message of identity, which is different than what God says about identity. Our music and movies dictate a false message of manhood and womanhood that we have adapted to the media culture without realizing how much impact it has left in our lives or even in our generation.

When we talk about turning our pain into purpose, we have to know and fully understand that only God can make beautiful things out of the things we call ugly. Out of the dust, he created us and did not see a mistake in his creation. Only God can make beauty out of the miseries that we are in. For a long time, I tried to do things on my own and tried to figure them out on my own. At some point, I got tired and said God, here I am. What's next? At some point, I had to surrender to God, and when I did that, I realized the very things that I was looking for were all in the hands of God. A Peace that passes all understanding, a joy that is unexplainable, and accessing freedom that the world can't ever provide. Surrendering to God's ways will elevate you to levels that you never thought you would be elevated to. The process of surrendering is going to require action from us, which is being vulnerable. God knows and sees all things and knows the mess that we are in; however, in the process of surrendering, we have to cast the burden on God.

A load of life is not meant to be carried upon our shoulders. I remember when I fully surrendered to

God was 2006. I was tired of going to the hospital week after week, day after day, and month after month. The damage that the epilepsy was causing to my life was so strong that the doctors had to tell my parents that if I ever wanted to be epilepsy free, I would need to have open-head surgery. Thank God for my family, who have faith in God and believe that I will be epilepsy free.

I went to the altar and told God, *"If this is your will for my life for me to have epilepsy forever, I will then have it. If it's not your will for my life to have epilepsy, I am asking God for freedom; I am asking God for healing. God, I am tired of going back and forth to the hospital and hearing news after news. I am tired of taking 03 pills twice a day, consuming 600 mg. God, each pill is 100 mg, and consuming 4200 mg in a week is too much. I am tired, God, and I am surrendering to this. In your word, God, it says, If you have faith as small as a mustard seed, I can tell this mountain to move from here to there, and it shall move. God, I am asking for this mountain of my life to be moved. Thank you in advance for your healing, thank you in advance for your miracle, Thank you in advance for your freedom."*

A month later, I had a seizure at an all-you-can-eat buffet resultant in Burien, WA. I had to go to the hospital, and while in the hospital bed, I heard a loud voice saying, *"you're delivered."* I truly believed the voice that I heard was God's voice. I went home and took all my epilepsy medication to the trash. My mother kept on refiling, and I kept on throwing them away.

From 2006 to the present, I am not in medications, and I am epilepsy free. The doctor's reports said one thing, but God's report said another thing. I understood this was not the final chapter of my life; therefore, I had to surrender to God, who is the God of victory. I had to surrender to the God who has my life mapped out from the beginning to the end. I had to surrender to believe that he would restore the things which looked like they were going to be defeated. What are you holding onto that you're not willing to Surender? What is in the way for God to do what he can do in your life? What is the thing in your life that you know it's killing you on the inside, and you want freedom from that thing, but you're just holding onto it, not doing anything good but killing you? Let go and let God and let him have his way in us and through us. The third thing that we must do to turn our pain into purpose is listed below.

Forgiveness

The word *forgiveness* has been viewed as a curse in the culture today, as if one does not deserve to be forgiven because of what they have done to us. We fail to realize that forgiveness plays a big role in our healing process but also when it comes to walking into our purpose. However, forgiveness has been overlooked as if it doesn't have a purpose. We have to fully understand without forgiveness, all we are doing is killing ourselves.

Unforgiveness is like drinking toxic and hoping that the other person dies. There is power in forgiving, there is growth in forgiving, and there is maturity in letting it go. I know it's easy to say, but it's hard to do. I truly believe the reason why forgiveness is so hard is that we have adapted to a hurting culture that says, if you do me wrong, I will do you wrong too. We've adapted to a culture that says an eye for an eye and a tooth for a tooth. We no longer talk about what hurt us and how someone impacted us negatively; instead, we turn to causing harm because they caused us harm without realizing the ripple effect behind it. I am a firm believer that hurt people will hurt people but healed people heal people. We are supposed to spread healing and not spread hurt. We are supposed to spread love and not spread the pain. We are supposed to spread authenticity and not duplicate what God did not create us to be.

Forgiveness is the key to the healing process. And forgiveness is the key when we talk about elevating our purpose. A lot of us have people in our lives that have done us wrong where; that hurt turned into pain, and that pain turned into a stronghold. Instead of us living life, the stronghold is living out our lives.

Instead of us stepping into what God has for us, the stronghold is holding us back, and no matter how far we go, we will find ourselves back at the same spot. Unforgiveness is like a boomerang. It can only go so far until it has to come back to where it started. So many times, we are like boomerangs where we try to go far in life and try to do all this just to find ourselves at the same spot where we started. Forgiveness has not something to do with the other person, but it has something to do with you as an individual. If you want to heal, you have to forgive transparently. Transparent forgiveness does not say that I have to let you back in my corner. The book of life says, "Bad company ruins good character" (1st Corinthians 15:33). Just because I forgive you, it does not mean I have to let you in my life. Just because I forgive you, it does not mean that I have to keep on accepting the damages that you're causing me over and over and over again. When we hear forgiveness, we have a tendency to think that because we forgive someone, we have to allow them to come back into our lives. If it costs your peace, it's too expensive. What are you holding onto that you refuse to let go of?

Many of us have wounds and scars from people who did us wrong. We are going through life and not realizing the very thing that is killing us on the inside is the very thing that we must let go of just so we can step into the next level and leave the bad seeds behind. What if the reason why you can bare no fruit in the seeds that you're planting is that you haven't forgiven yet what hurt you? What if the reason why we find ourselves back at the same spot over and over again is that we haven't healed what made us bleed? What if the reason why we can't see an answered prayer is that we're refusing to let go? What if letting go would be the answered prayer you need the whole time? One thing about the hurts and wounds is if they do not get addressed when they are small, they will age up with us, and the more they age, the worst they get. Every time we step into a new chapter of life, that thing is coming with us in the new chapter. If we don't cut that branch, that branch will grow and will take root, which will cause you to bleed on people who didn't do anything wrong to you. If we don't address the forgiveness aspect, we will keep going through life with triggers, wounds, and scars, and it will take us back to the moment of time when a certain situation rose.

When we talk about moving forward and stepping into our purpose and turning the pain into purpose, we have to fully understand that forgiveness is a big step into walking into purpose. We have to understand that we will never be able to walk into what is in store for us if we are going to hold on to what has been killing us. I know it's painful, I know it's hard, I know it's frustrating, I know your mind and thought process is having all these wishes of what you want to see happen to the person who did wrong to you. That still won't change the deep wounds that have been rooted. The process of forgiveness is going to require us to take action to do the healing process. If the healing process means going to see a therapist, please do just that. Whatever you do, don't quit, don't bend, and don't fold because there is more in you than what you think. Whatever you do, don't throw in the towel because there is beauty that will come out of the very thing that you're in at the current moment. One of the biggest poisons in my life that I had to come face to face with was the father's wound. Healing from this father's wound took a toll on me and impacted me negatively when it came to building and establishing relationships. I was walking toxic without even realizing how toxic I was. I was putting the blame on others when they didn't do anything wrong to me. I was trying to fill this void that no man can't fulfill but God.

It wasn't until I went to go see a therapist and addressed everything to my therapist and told her where I was at, my thought process, and my brokenness. Session after session, it was getting better and better. Until one session came up, and my therapist told me to look in the mirror. I looked in the mirror, and she said, "You're a reflection of your parent's seed. When you plant your own seed, it will be a reflection of you. You have two options. To repeat the cycle or defeat the cycle. You have two options to make excuses or bring a solution. If you want to keep making excuses, you're going to find yourself repeating these hurts to your legacy. If you want to make a solution, you have to be able to forgive what has caused you pain. You have to be able to transparently forgive what you can't change." I looked at my therapist, and I cried, I wept, I shed tears. I told her, How can I transparently forgive? She said, first, you must give it to God; second, you need to attack the giant because you're not defeated; you're a conqueror and someone who is victorious. If victory is what you want, giving it to God and forgiving are the steps you must take. Was it easy? No. But was it rewarding? Yes. I did just that. I gave it to God, and I forgave my father for a wound that started when I was five years old. I had to come to the realization that I can't change what happened in the past, but I can make sure what happened in the past does not get carried on forward. I had to realize that my holding onto this big deep father wound would not better me but instead kill me.

It was Father's day of 2022; my wife and I left the church, and the preacher was talking about forgiving your fathers and letting the grudge go. I couldn't fully be available for my wife, who was my fiancé at the time, because of my father's wound. My wife needed me to be present and needed me to be the best version of myself, so she was willing to hear my hurt, listen to my cries, and just be fully present. When you have people who leave your life when things get difficult, it's hard to open up, and sometimes you feel the best option to do is to hush. My wife was consistently present in every aspect. She was also present when I went to go forgive my father. After church that day, she and I went to my mom's house, and usually, every fathers day, I always tell my mom *Happy Mothers' Day* and give her a gift. But this time, this wasn't the case. The message that my pastor preached on that Sunday for fathers day convicted me that I had to forgive what I can no longer accept and take with me to the next level. While I was at my mom's house, my younger brother asked me if I had told my dad *Happy Fathers' Day.*

Immediately, I had the same response every time. That's not my dad; that's your dad. After I said that, I was convicted, and I took the step to forgive. I went to my car and grabbed this fresh box of cologne that I had bought months ago that I had never used. It was still in the box, never opened. I went and gave him this expensive cologne and told him *Happy Father's Day.* This is where things started to get real.

While my wife, my brothers, and my mom were in the house, I told my dad I needed to talk to him outside, just him and me. I told him that I love him, and I told him *Thank You* for teaching us how to focus on God and know God for ourselves. While I gave him his applause, I also told him the hurt. I told him that we may not have had the best relationship growing up because I didn't view him as a father. When you told us to never call you dad, you're not our dad to call you pastor, I ran with that. From five years old to twenty-eight years old, I never called you dad. For twenty-three years, I never called you dad. I don't even know what your hugs feel like. I never even heard you tell me you love me and you're proud of me. We never have a father and son time, and when I see other kids with their dads, I get sad because I wish that was me. Your absence left a big wound on me.

I need to let this pain go, and I am telling you that I forgive you because my legacy needs to be healed. My wife needs me healed. This is impacting our relationship, and I am not going to lose my wife because I am broken. Dad, I forgive you. While tears were coming down my face and we were hugging each other, I told him, dad, this is my first time hugging you. For twenty-eight years of my life, I have never hugged you, and I am just now hugging you.

I cried so much to the point where you can hear every age me up to twenty-eight was crying. The five-year-old me was crying because the five-year-old me was looking for affection. The five-year-old was looking for a dad. The five-year-old me was holding things in while the pain was increasing over and over, being told to just be silent. The ten-year-old me was crying because the ten-year-old wanted my father's blessings. To be heard, loved, and appreciated.

Instead, it was pain, neglect, and rejection. When I forgave my father, he heard the five-year-old me speak, the ten-year-old me spoke, the seventeen-year-old me spoke, the 21-year-old me spoke, and the 28-year-old me speak. He heard the stages of pain that were carrying on since the age of five when he told his kids, *"Never call me dad. I am not your dad. Call me Pastor."*

I released so much on that Father's day, and the tears couldn't stop shedding. I let everything go, and when I let it go, I started to glow. My mom was crying, my wife was crying, and my little brother was crying because they heard so much pain that was built inside, which they didn't know was still inside. I knew If I didn't make the decision to forgive, this hurt would have been carried onto my legacy and my own seeds.

I didn't want to carry this down my bloodline, so therefore I drew a line in the sand and said, today is the day that I will be free and release what needs to be released. Today is the day that I will step into the next season, embracing my freedom and releasing the bondage and strongholds. I was serious about my healing because it didn't do any good keeping it in. I was able to forgive even when an apology wasn't even offered. When you're able to forgive when there wasn't a request for an apology, that speaks maturity. Today, I am able to be the best version of myself for my wife. She had seen a version of me that she didn't see before because now I am healed, and before, I was still in pain. My question for you is, how serious are you about your healing? How serious are you about your purpose? How serious are you about doing something different? There is someone who looks at you as a role model, someone who looks up to you as inspiration.

You may not know who you're inspiring, who you're impacting, and who you're influencing. But know this, someone is always watching even when you think they are not watching. How you move can shape how they move. There is a message in the midst of brokenness, and there's healing even in the midst of the storms.

What if the reason why the best you can't manifest is because of things that you have not forgiven? What if the answered prayer you're looking for manifests when you truly forgive? Turning your pain into purpose is going to require you to forgive and ask God for the strength to forgive. You felt hurt; now you got to face the hurt. But when you face the hurt, don't face it with a reaction of violence but face it with the reaction of forgiveness. Face it, feel it, and forgive it. The fourth thing that we must do to turn our pain into purpose is listed below.

Love You How God Loves You

When trials of life come, the first thing we do is question everything about us. We question our worth, we question if we have been validated, we question the purpose of why we are here, and we also question if, at times, we are loved. Instead of us asking, God, what Is it that you are trying to show me, the first thing we do is go straight to victimized mode and think of the worst of the worst.

When we talk about turning our pain into purpose, we first have to understand that we must love ourselves first before we can love others. We can only love others in the same measure that we love ourselves. When we realize what true love is about, we will then be awoken to the fact what God says is love is different from what the world says is love.

The foundation of your blossoming starts with self-care. The foundation of your bringing impact starts with self-development. The foundation of your turning your mess into a message and turning your test into a testimony starts with God being in the driver's seat and understanding how he loves you. When we fully understand how much love God has for us, we will then walk this walk in the measurement of the love that God has for us. I can remember I was searching for love in different ways because I had a father wound where I didn't get love from my own father. I can remember that I was struggling with identity issues because of my father's wound. I was looking for love in the wrong places because I didn't have a reflection of what love was all about.

I didn't know how to love myself because I never felt validated by my father. I never felt validated; therefore, I felt like there wasn't any value that I could pour out into the world. I didn't know I was someone of value because of a lack of validation. It wasn't until I really got into the word and truly surrendered to God that I noticed what God considers love is not what the world considers love.

I remember reading his word, and tears flowed down my eyes, and I started feeling a change on the inside and being wrapped in his arms. The first time I was wrapped in the arms of God, I said this is it. That was when I knew God was real for me. I started proclaiming and declaring what God says about me and not what the world says about me. I started changing my affirmations from negative to positive because I knew he was the king of love. The more I rested in his presence, the more I was consumed and wrapped in his arms.

The more I was in his presence, the more I was validated and had the strength to love myself. When we talk about turning pain into passion, we have to understand that in order for passion to manifest, love has to be present. We can't just make moves to make moves, but we have to make moves that will push toward purpose. If it's not purpose-driven moves, I don't want to make that move.

When I started embracing the love of God, my thought process and how I responded started to change. I want you to know that even in the midst of pain, you can still love yourself. Even in the midst of trials and tribulations, you can still love yourself. Even in the midst of whatever it is that you're facing or going through, you can still love yourself. Even in the midst of whatever it may be, you can still root and cheer for yourself.

If you don't know how to love yourself, you will never know how to love others. If you don't know how to love others, you will never be able to establish a solid relationship with other people. God is the masterpiece of love, and he is the masterpiece of our lives, and he has everything all set from the beginning to the end. I understand that at times you don't feel like you're worthy of being loved, but I want you to know before you even face the storms you're currently facing, God already said it was finished when he sent his son to die on the cross. Because of God's love, I am soaring like an eagle and not soaring like a crow. Because of God's love, the fruits that I reap are different because God is in the driver's seat in whatever I am doing. Because of God's love, I can go day by day and week by week and tell people firmly with confidence that purpose is attached to you, destiny is attached to you, breaking cycles is attached to you, and being a generational blessing is attached to you.

When you love yourself how God loves you, the only thing you can do is love others how God loves you. Love has to be the equation and the center. But in order for it to be the equation and in the center, it's going to require God to be in the center of it all. How much do you love yourself? How much do you spend time with yourself? Turning your pain into passion is going to require you to love in order for passion to manifest.

It's going to require you to love how God loves you in order to bare the fruit that God has in store for you. Loving you is going to require you to watch what you declare out of your mouth. Loving you is going to require you to be careful with what you watch with your eyes. Loving you is going to require you to not put your peace on the line. You're loved, you're destined with love, and before you were pushed out of your mother's womb, love was attached to you. If you want to grow, you must love yourself the way God loves you. If you want to leave an impact, you must love yourself how God loves you. And if you want to break cycles, you must love yourself how God loves you. Without love, the answer will always be hate. But with love, the answer will always be love. The last thing that we must do in order for us to turn our pain into passion is listed below.

Let Go And Let God

One of the biggest questions people have always asked me is, How are you able to do what you're doing? How are you able to do this at a young age? How are you so determined? My immediate response is to let go and let God. Turning your pain into purpose is going to require us to let go of ourselves and put God in the driver's seat. God used what I thought was useless and turned it into something powerful.

God used what I thought was purposeless and made it purposeful. God used what I thought would be impossible to turn it around and make it possible. When we talk about turning our pain into purpose, we have to be able to let go of what we can't control and trust God will do the rest. You are never too old or too young to be used by God. Man disqualifies you, but God qualifies the disqualified. The world will look at your mess and say no potential. But God could look at your mess and says, that's potential. The world can look at your track record and label you as such, but God can look at your track record and don't label you as such. The world can look at your upbringing and say this is it, but God can look at your upbringing and say, this is not over. I want you to fully know and understand what the world says about your life and your future is different than what God says about your life and your future.

Many of us are looking to be qualified in the eyes of many, but I want you to understand if you're looking for qualification from a man, you will always be disqualified. But God is the one that calls the unqualified, qualified. Despite your shortcomings and downfalls and etc., God qualifies the unqualified. Throughout the Bible, we can see different people who God has used who we may say were not qualified to do the work whatsoever.

David was a small boy but defeated Goliath and became a king. In the David and Goliath story, we have to understand that David was not trained or equipped for the battleground. Goliath was a giant philistine who was undefeated. In the man's view, we will say David is about to get beat up. In the lens of man, we will say, according to his record, David does not know how to fight. According to his record, he is not trained for this fight. We might even be the ones to tell David to stop what he is doing because he is going against a Giant. David had no earthly idea of what it meant to be important but instead had a heart that was willing to listen to God. David didn't go into battle with the lens of the flesh; he went into battle with the lens of the spirit. In 1st Samuel 17:43, we see that Goliath said to David, "Am I a dog, that you come at me with sticks?

He went on in 17:44 and said, "I'll give your flesh to the birds and the wild animals."

It's important we see the response to what David told Goliath. David said in 17:45-47, "You come against me with sword and spear and javelin, but I come against you in the name of the Lord Almighty, the God of the armies of Israel, whom you have defied. This day the Lord will deliver you into my hands, and I'll strike you down and cut off your head. This very day I will give the carcasses of the Philistine army to the birds and the wild animals, and the whole world will know that there is a God in Israel. All those gathered here will know that it is not by sword or spear that the Lord saves; for the battle is the Lord's, and he will give all of you into our hands." Goliath depended on his own strength, and David depended on God. David knew this fight was not his fight; this fight belonged to the Lord.

There are some battles that we are facing, and we are trying to overcome them in our own might; we have to fully understand this fight does not belong to us. It belongs to the Lord. We have to be able to let go and let God so God can do what he needs to do. We see that God used Peter, who was a poor fisherman but became a disciple and a fisher of men (Matthew 4:19). We see that God used Esther, who was born in Exile, and a woman at the time who was a second-class citizen but saved the Jews (Esther 8:1-17). We see

Joseph, who was a carpenter but was chosen to be the stepfather of Jesus — raising the son of man in humility (Matthew 13:55). We see Mary, who was a teenager but trusted to be the mother of a man destined to die for the world to live (Luke 1:30).

None of these people were prepared to do what God had planned for them, yet they were chosen anyways. None of these people were equipped, but they were chosen anyways. Do not let what you're in make you believe that this is it for you. Do not let what you are facing to make you believe you're not fit to do what needs to be done. Despite the imperfections, God can still use you in a mighty way, and we have to be able to trust and rest in God. The Bible is full of stories of people who were used by God despite their unfaithfulness and failures. There's a story of Abraham, the one who would be later known as the father of the nation of Israel. Abraham's life was far from perfect. At one point, he and his wife, Sarah, doubted God and tried to fulfill the promise by having a child through the woman Hagar (Genesis 16:3-16).

Despite this, God gave Abraham and Sarah Issac, who would then later on, after many generations, resulting in the nation of Israel. We see Samson. Out of all the men that God would use in the old testament, I don't think there was anyone more hard-headed and arrogant than Samson. But even with that, God would give him supernatural strength through the power of the holy spirit. We have Moses, who was a prince of Egypt, but he was also a coward and a murderer. After having killed an Egyptian (Exodus 2:12).

He fled to the location he fled to, only to be called there by God in the form of a burning bush. Moses also had speech problems or at least the confidence to speak publicly, but God gave him Aaron so that he would fulfill God's purpose by freeing the people of Israel from the corrupt rule of Egypt and by leading them to the promised land. Then we have Peter. Peter, who was once called Simon. Peter was one of Jesus' disciples who would, later on, become one of the apostles of the early church. Peter wasn't always bold, but he was always impulsive and often acted before thinking. At one point, Jesus was being tried, and Peter denied Christ three times. But he would later be restored by Jesus back into ministry and would be filled with the Holy Spirit, becoming an anointed apostle of the church who did mighty miracles and preached powerfully in public. It does not matter what situation you're in and what you're facing; God can still use you mightily.

In 1st Corinthians chapter 1:26-31, it says in the message version, "Take a good look, friends, at who you were when you got called into this life. I don't see many of "the brightest and the best" among you, not many influential, not many from high-society families. Isn't it obvious that God deliberately chose men and women that the culture overlooks and exploits and abuses, choosing these *nobodies* to expose the hollow pretensions of the *somebodies*?

That makes it quite clear that none of you can get by with blowing your own horn before God. Everything that we have — right thinking and right living, a clean slate, and a fresh start — comes from God by way of Jesus Christ. That's why we have the saying, "if you're going to blow a horn, blow a trumpet for God." Turning your pain into purpose is going to require you to believe that what we can see as impossible, God can make possible. Just like how God used people who were not qualified, prepared, or trained to do what needed to be done, God can use you in the same way and in the same manner. I understand it can be hard to let go because we don't know about the unknown. And we have become people who want to know the unknown. What is going to happen next? That in itself can be very scary in trying to understand what is going to happen next since we don't know.

I am always reminded of the story of when Jesus was asleep on the boat, and the disciples were afraid. There wasn't any reason why they should be afraid. They walked with Christ, and they have seen the work that Christ was doing, but they still missed it. I realize at times, in letting Go and letting God, God could do wonders and miracles in our lives, but we can still miss it and not understand it.

We can still miss the fact that if God can do it before, he can surely do it again. I truly believe that in Mark 4:35-41, Jesus opens the disciples to the frightening possibility, and they are wrong. I truly believe that Jesus has the same message for us today, which is "Peace. Be still! Jesus was asleep on a cushion, and the storm was coming, and the disciples woke him up and asked, "Teacher, don't you care if we drown?" The Gospel of Mark then states that he woke up and rebuked the wind, and said to the sea, "Peace! Be still!" I truly believe it's very important for us to know and understand that in the process of letting go and letting God, there are going to be some questions that will happen because we want to know what will happen next. When we talk about turning your pain into purpose, there are going to be times of trying to figure out what is the unknown, and we have to just trust and rest assured in the hands of God that things will be still. We have to be confident firmly through it all that God will be with us every step of the way. Despite the storms, despite the obstacle, despite the trials and tribulations, we have to be able to say, God, it's in your hands.

The importance of leaving it to the hands of God is that he has the master plan of life and knows all things because he is all-knowing. If God sends you to it, he will get you through it. I have seen over and over again how God got me through the obstacles and the tragedies of life just for me to be an impact and a vessel to hundreds of people. I let go of what people said, and I hold on to what God says because of that; if there is any unknown that I may have, I leave it to the hands of God to take care of it. Let go and let God is the key when turning your pain into passion. There is a jewel behind the mess, there's a jewel behind your story, and there's a jewel behind whatever you're encountering.

Whatever you do, make sure your faith in Christ does not waver so that when the wind of life moves left and right, you won't be moved. Through it all, there's the motivation that happens from the mess. Through it all, there's a motivation that happens behind the pain. Let the hurt teach you but let the pain motivate you.

Chapter 7 — Motivation Behind The Pain

In life, we have the option to either repeat the cycle or do something different about it. In life, we have the option to either let that pain motivate us to do something different or just dwell in the pain of what is going on. Through all of these life obstacles and seeing how my pain was turning into purpose, and doing the steps that I listed in the last chapter to turn the pain into purpose, a lot of great things happened and took place in my life.

Through it all, I give God all the honor and all the glory for it. Many people don't see behind-the-scenes work, but they see what is happening in the front of the scenes. Many people see the awards and the accolades but don't see the struggle through it all. I wrote this book because I wanted people to be motivated and inspired to stay in the course even when it's difficult.

I want people to understand that they need to take control of the pen and create something out of nothing. I want people to understand that if you know how it tastes like, do what you need to do to make sure it's not repeated. When I realized the burning passion in me was stirring, and it manifested before my eyes, I was determined to keep on going and going after what it was that God still had in store for me. I was motivated by the pain of the father's wound, and now

I mentor kids who are fatherless. I coached kids who were fatherless. Giving them hope to stay on the course even when it's hard and difficult.

As someone who felt the pain of neglect, rejection, and abandonment, I now go to schools that reach out to me to talk to their kids and youth. I share my story because I am healed, and I am not ashamed of my story because I know it can be an inspiration and motivation to someone else who might have encountered what I have encountered. I am not ashamed of my story because I want people to be healed and not stay in the mess that they are in. I am not ashamed of my story because I want people to be free.

We are made to be free; we are made to be in peace. And if we don't look at peace, we will find ourselves rested in peace; therefore, I have a duty to bring a message that will restore what was lost. I have a duty as a healed person to bring a message that will convict and help others take action so they can be a part of their own healing. Before, I thought everything was an accident, and the mess I was in was all an accident. Then I realized how much impact was left behind by the mess that I was in. I realize how my testimony gave others to not quit in the midst of their own test. I realize how my misery had turned into a ministry where now I am sharing the very things that are vulnerable just so I can meet someone else where they are at. The motivation behind the pain showed me there is purpose in the midst of pain. The motivation behind the pain showed me there is still a pang of hunger in the midst of pain. The motivation behind the pain shows me the reason why you got to fight is that the why is bigger than the excuse.

The reason why you got to fight is that someone who is connected to you needs to hear how you made it through. The motivation behind the pain showed me that all things work together for good. The thing about motivation is there has to be the inspiration, and without inspiration, there won't be any motivation. What motivates you to stay on the course? What motivates you to keep on keeping on?

Until I let go and let God, things were falling right into place. I want you to know behind the pain, there is a birth of motivation that will be released. Behind the pain, there is a jewel attached that can impact and touch nations. I was so motivated to leave an impact that media companies were reaching out to me for me to share my message. I didn't realize how big of an impact I was doing until I realized how much of an impact was left just because I let God do what he needed to do in my life and through my life. I could recall when my 2nd book came out, *"What is your Why Behind The Drive,"* a lot of people were telling me that my book was transforming lives like crazy. My immediate response was, that's cool, praise God.

People told me that someone passed my book to them, and it changed their life for the better good. It was reassuring to hear how life was impacted for the better good. It was reassuring to hear that I am where God needed me to be because if one life can be touched and impacted, my job is done. The motivation behind the pain was bearing fruit that I didn't even notice or see.

The last thing that reaps in a tree is the fruit. I was busy planting seeds that I didn't take the time to see the fruit that was being reaped behind the seeds that were being planted. I was getting calls left and right to speak at this school, this organization, this platform and etc., because of the impact of the pain, because of the inspiration that inspired many people to stay the course. The biggest eye-opener was when the media started reaching out. In 2021 that's when I started to see the fruit behind the labor throughout all them years. It felt like month after month, big publications were reaching out because the work that I was doing also impacted their region.

The amazing part about all this is the very thing that God showed me in 2006 was manifesting in my life in the year 2021. God had to do a work in me before he could do the work through me just so a positive impact could be left. I didn't know when I was going to manifest or touch what God showed me, but I just knew if I just stayed in the course and had a heart that was willing, he would do what he needed to do and how he needed to do it. Fifteen years from what God showed me to when it manifested was worth every single pain that I encountered. Not one thing that I have encountered where I said I regret going through it.

Because everything that I have gone through had a role in bettering me as an individual. Everything that I had gone through positioned me for something that God had in store for me. My pain is now my why, which is now my fuel to keep on keeping on. My pain has turned into my way to go back down the elevator and help someone else come up so they can see they don't have to stay where they are at. What is your pain causing you? Is it birthing something in you, or are you giving it the power to kill the very thing that is in you that needs to be released? The pain of life doesn't have power unless you give it the power to do what it needs to do, which is to kill you. Nobody has the power to destroy you unless you give it the power to destroy you.

Just because you look defeated does not mean that you're defeated. I want you to know and understand that you're not defeated; defeat is not part of your identity, but overcoming is a part of your identity. I want you to fully understand that overcoming is who you are, and the pain of life has one duty, which is to help you help others overcome what you have overcome.

The struggle of life is not for you, but it's for someone else with who you're connected to that needs to hear how you made it through. The motivation behind the pain is going to lead you to impact for the better good. In order to leave a good impact, you have to use your pain as motivation. We have to go through the process of healing so our pain can turn into purpose.

My motivation is to keep on keeping and be a light to others out there who may be on the edge of giving up because of the storms in their life. If I can go through it and grow through it, then you can too. Don't look at the pain as a downfall but look at the pain as a motivation to keep on keeping on. Whatever you don't quit, let it teach you what needs to be taught in that moment or even in that season. Whatever you don't fold because you're made and equipped for more. You never know who is watching you and who you're inspiring.

Just because you don't know it does not mean that there's not one person whose inspired by what you do. I remember my childhood friend that I grew up with in church name Quincy Wanzala told me when I was 18 years old that I have a voice and my voice will touch and impact lives from all over. He went on and told me to make sure that I am not silent because the enemy will try to silence my voice, so I don't bring forth the change that is needed in your city.

Those words he gave me stayed with me, and it was more of a confirmation than anything else. It was confirmation that I am where I needed to be and also confirmation that I am the voice that my generation needs to hear. It's a bold statement, but I truly believe wholeheartedly in that statement. I took so much pride in helping others bounce back from their setback to the point where I was hearing testimonies from others left and right on how their lives were changed.

I take joy when I hear that life was turned around for good. People have always asked me why I am not afraid of sharing my story. The reason why I am not afraid to share my story is that I am a healed man. Since I am a healed individual, my story will help others to heal, and that's why I share my story. I share my story because it's through the stories that healing begins for others, and we're made to be healed and not made to be broken. I want people to understand just because it might look like things are falling apart, it does not mean that you're falling apart. In the midst of chaos, you still have a purpose. In the midst of trials and tribulations, you still have a purpose. If broken crayons can still color, then you can keep on going even in the midst of the brokenness. Do not allow the brokenness of life to make you believe that you don't have a purpose of keeping on going. Do not allow the shatters of life to make you believe that you no longer have value. Because you have value, the attack on life will be much stronger.

Because you have value, the enemy will do whatever to make sure you don't believe you're valuable. After I learned how to turn my pain into purpose, I was then motivated by the pain, which now produces purpose-driven results. I am not just making moves to make moves, but I make moves that leave an impact. My question for you is, what is your motivation behind the pain? There are less than 24 hours in a day; how are you letting that pain that bothers you motivate you to be a part of the solution?

One of my biggest mentors is Les Brown. Since I was a kid, I have looked up to Les Brown because he was already on the platform that I wanted to be on. Les and I had a lot of things in common. We both were told we weren't going to amount to anything, we both were in special education, and because of the limitations that people have seen, they gave up on us because of the setbacks.

I remember going to every *"Get Motivated"* event where he was the keynote speaker. One of the things he always says is, *"You've got to be hungry."* He talked about when he got to the radio, and even when he was rejected, he came back requesting to be aired. Everyone said no because of what they saw, but Les saw something different.

He saw the potential and the possibilities, while others saw the impossibilities. The more I went to go see him live at the event, the more the fire in me kept on going higher and higher. I was able to connect with Les Brown, and his story gave me hope and reassurance that if he can do it, I can do it. I was hungry to touch nations, I was hungry to break the odds that were thrown my way, and I was hungry to see life change for the good. I was hungry to break the cycle. I can either let what is going on make me or break me. I can either make excuses or get a solution. I chose to be a part of the solution. I want to show others with disabilities that the dreams they have can still step in them.

I wanted to show others who had an IEP (Individual Education Plan) that how it looks doesn't mean that is how it's going to finish. You just have to a why that is bigger than your excuses so you can go after it no matter what. My message started spreading like fire throughout the town. I wasn't only viewed as the person who was a poet and motivational speaker, but I was also viewed by the community as the person who was breaking the odds that were thrown his way. The message then spread throughout different states. I then found my calendar being booked for events to speak at local and state-wide conferences to inspire others to keep on keeping on. My pain turned into my passion which became my motivation to go throughout and share a message that will help the hopeless to become hopeful despite how it looks. If we can use a rip dollar bill to get what we want from the store, then we can use our brokenness to change narratives in our lives. If we want a wrinkled dollar, a torn apart dollar because the value of the dollar doesn't change, then the value in our lives don't change just because we are ripped or torn. Les showed me if you're not hungry for what you say you want to see manifest in your life, then you will never get it. If you're not motivated to change the cycle of your life, then it just won't change. If you're not taking the action that is needed to be a part of the solution, you will then keep on repeating the same cycle.

The number one competition that we have is not the one to the left and right of us, but it's the one you see in the mirror on a daily basis. When you look in the mirror, what do you see? Do you see someone of value? Or do you see someone with no value? Do you see someone of worth? Or do you see someone who is not of worth? How you view yourself will play a role in the level of hunger you have to see effective change happen. The message that I was spreading came back to the people who counted me out. The same people who counted me out are the same people who are reaching out to me today, asking me to facilitate or do a workshop at their school or facility. The same people who have told me that I won't amount to anything because of epilepsy are the same people who are calling me today to tell me how their lives have changed because I didn't fold when it was difficult. They call me to tell me how my why motivates them to stay on the course even though it's difficult. My question for you is, how hungry are you? How determined are you? How motivated are you? Are you hungry enough to throw your excuses away just so your why can manifest into flames that will position you toward your purpose? We may not know what doors are going to be opened just because we choose to stay the course. I didn't know what was going to happen next, but I trusted God that he would do what he said he would do. When God says it, it will come to fruition.

It may not happen when we want it to happen; however, when he does it in his timing, he will do it exceedingly and abundantly. Whatever that pain is, turn it into purpose so then you can be motivated to leave an imprint that was designed for you to leave the way God intended it for you to leave. There is a message behind the pain which can lead to motivation to create a powerful change. Don't ignore your pain but take action to heal so then your pain can bring effective change. You're made to heal, you're made to bring impact, and you're made to be the best version of yourself. There are no limits attached to you, be limitless in all that you do, and the things you didn't see coming will start manifesting. Let that pain be the fuel to keep on keeping on keeping on. Let that pain be the motivation to endure the race even when you feel like you can't endure anymore. In all that you do, make sure you stand. If you fall, get back up. You can fall, but you can't fold. You can fall, but you got to rise up and keep on going. Someone is counting on you, your seed is counting on you, your legacy is counting on you, and whatever you do, you can't afford to quit.

The only thing you can afford to do is keep on striving through it all because you're made to win. Let the pain motivate you, but in the midst of the pain, you got to believe there's a purpose in pain. You got to start looking at the glass half full instead of empty. You got to be able to have faith as small as a mustard seed to believe there's something good coming out in the midst of the pain. In order to have that belief mindset, we have to obtain a winning mindset.

Chapter 8 — Winning Mindset

One of the biggest questions people have always asked is, how do I win? How am I supposed to trust and have faith that everything is going to be alright when it seems like it will never happen to me? How am I supposed to be reassured that everything is going to be alright when It's not looking alright? How do you want me to trust that it's possible when it seems impossible? In life, it's never about what you're going through, but it's about how we respond to what we are going through.

Everything we go through has a plan attached to it. It has one mission which is to push us toward our purpose. In a world that speaks negativity, it becomes easy to believe in the negative and not the positive. It's easy to believe what can't be done instead of what can be done. Henry Ford once said, *"Whether you think you can or think you can't, you're right."*

A lot of times, we believe or think that we cannot because of our environment and also what others have spoken into our lives. It's important to know and fully understand that you're not a product of your environment, and just because how it started looks ugly does not mean how it needs to finish has to stay ugly. I always say behind every mess, there's a message; behind every test, there's a testimony; and behind every misery, there's a ministry. Nothing about what you face in life is an accident, and God can use what we may seem purposeless and make it purposeful. God can use what we may call worthless and turn it around and show us how it was worth it.

When we talk about establishing a winning mindset and what that entails, we have to first understand that believing is the foundation behind everything. We have to first understand that without believing, a foundation can not be established. A winning mindset requires a couple of things from us. It will be provided below.

Changing The Affirmations Spoken

If we want to have a winning mindset, it's going to require changing what we are declaring over our lives. It's going to require us to be intentional with what's being spoken out of our mouths. Lisa M Hayes once said, "Be careful how you're talking to yourself because you're listening."

The words that we speak over our lives will determine the mindset that we will carry on every single day. Our words are like boot camp. Boot camp trains you and equips you with what you need to know before it's time for whatever it could be. When we think of military boot camp, we think of the intensive training that comes into effect before it's time to go out and fight. How you train will determine how you perform when it's time for the battleground. And if you don't take boot camp training seriously, then you're not ready when it's time for war. It's the same when we talk about the words that we are declaring over our lives. If all we do is speak garbage over our lives and let others speak garbage into our lives, when the trials and tribulations of life come, we will find ourselves declaring what we have been planting over our lives for a long time.

The words that we affirm our lives with will determine the mentality that we will carry every single day. What songs are you singing on your radio station? What affirmations are you declaring over your life? Based on those affirmations, what is the effect it has on your life? We fail to realize that lot of times, why we can't win because we have downloaded so much garbage into our lives that victory will look like it's impossible because we have planted seeds of affirmations that are destructible instead of seeds of affirmations that are unstoppable.

We have planted seeds of affirmations that will make us believe it's impossible instead of seeds of affirmations that will make us believe it's possible in the midst of what may seem impossible. A winning mindset requires us to believe we can, we must, and we will, even in the midst of setbacks. A winning mindset requires us to look beyond what the storm is and not speak defeat but speak victory.

When you're able to have affirmations of positivity and declare what God says about you and not what man says about you, you will start to believe that in the midst of what you're in, you will bounce back from the setbacks. When you start declaring the affirmations of who God says you're, you will start looking at the mountains of your life and speak life and victory to those mountains because you're connected to God, who could move the mountains.

A winning mindset requires you to change your radio station because not every song needs to be sung and not every word needs to be declared, and not every message needs to be planted. If you want to win, it's going to require us to be intentional with what's being planted. How serious are you with winning in the seasons of your life? How hungry are you to see victory manifest in your life? How committed are you to winning for your family, for your legacy, and for your community? If you're serious, it's going to require you to take the next step listed below.

Fight Even When You Can't Fight No More

If you want a winning mindset, you have to be able to stay in the course even when the course may seem difficult. You have to be able to press and push even when you feel like you're at your breaking point. The thing about being a winner is that it's going to require a fight in you that must be released. When I say fight, I am not talking about a physical fight.

However, I am talking about the fight to keep on going when it seems like you can't go more. I am talking about the fight to be better than the day before because the competition is not with the person on the left or right of you, but it's with the person in the mirror. A winning mindset requires you to stay in the fight in the midst of being knocked down. Just because it looks like defeat, it does not mean you're defeated.

Just because it looks impossible, it doesn't mean that it is impossible. Just because it looks like there's no way out, it doesn't mean there's no way out. A winner understands that no matter how much they get knocked down in the midst of the setback, they know and fully understand what's coming behind this setback, positioning them for the bounce back. It might look ugly right now, and it might taste like defeat right now, but it does not mean that it's over. You have to be willing to fight in the midst even when you feel like you can't fight anymore. In order to have a winning mindset, you have to look at the storms of life with the lens of Christ and not look at the storms of life with the lens of the flesh. What are you saying? When David had to go against Goliath, if he had looked at Goliath through the lens of the flesh, he may not go against Goliath. Goliath was a giant, an undefeated philistine who didn't lose to anybody.

Fighting is Goliath, equipped to fight is Goliath; looking at the size and the resumè of David and Goliath, it makes sense in the physical lens to say David is about to be defeated. It makes sense in the physical lens to tell David, don't go against this Philistine. David was a king, but he was not prepared for war. He had no fighting experience, not equipped to fight whatsoever, but one thing he didn't do was doubt that he would be victorious.

The difference between David and Goliath was this. Goliath depended on his own strength, and David depended on God's strength. When God fights the battles, victory is what will be attached. My question for you is, who is fighting your battles? Who's in the driver's seat of your battles? Are you drowning in your own strength to get the victory, or are you depending on the God who is the God of victory? I could remember being in and out of the hospital for the first 13 years of my life fighting this fight against epilepsy. I was in the hospital week after week, day after day, not knowing what the final outcome might be. This fight against epilepsy was so heavy that I couldn't be left unattended because it could happen at any point and time. I am thankful that my parents taught me how to fight for my breakthrough, how to press for my breakthrough, and how to look at God for my breakthrough and not look at the report.

If I had looked at the report, I would have believed that it was the final report. But because I know there's victory in Christ, I pressed for my breakthrough by fighting on my knees because that's how winners win the battle. In order to have a winning mindset, we have to be able to let God be God and trust and believe what he said will come to pass.

The last time I had a seizure was in October of 2006. In November of 2006, I was in a hospital bed, and the doctors didn't understand what had changed in their system. I heard a loud voice telling me I was delivered, and I had faith as small as a mustard seed, believing the voice I was hearing was the voice of God. With that faith, I went home and took all my medications, and threw it all in the trash. My mother kept refilling the medications, and I kept throwing them away. From 2006 to the present, I never had a seizure ever again. In order to have a winning mindset, we have to understand not every fight needs to be fought and let God fight those battles. When I was serious about winning, I was committed to letting God be the driver's seat of everything. I have tried to do things on my own, and it was an epic fail. I was trying to bare the fruits with my own might and strength and realized it was not possible.

But when I let God fight my battles, and I placed him in the driver's seat of my life, I started to reap the overflow. It got hard, but I pressed through the mark. There was a reassurance that everything was going to be alright when I let it be in the hands of God. I started stepping into the overflow of things, and things started opening left and right because I let the God of purpose be in control of my purpose.

I started to get big publications reaching out to me, such as Yahoo Finance, New York Weekly, The American Reporter, and much more. When I was trying to fight in my own might, I wanted to quit and doubt everything. But when I placed God in the driver's seat, things fell right into place. Winning mindset not just fights, but they also understand what they are fighting and who they are fighting. Ephesians 6:12 says, "For we are not fighting against flesh-and-blood enemies, but against evil rulers and authorities of the unseen world, against mighty powers in this dark world, and against evil spirits in the heavenly places." It's important for us to truly understand who the battle is with. What are we fighting? Why are we fighting, and who are we fighting? A winning mindset requires staying on guard and on post through it all. It requires us to be steadfast and unmovable. The next steps to a winning mindset are listed below.

Surround Yourself With Winners

If you want to win, it's going to require you to surround yourself with other winners. If you want to be the best, you have to surround yourself with and learn from the best. So many times, we get mad and frustrated because we see the fruits that are being bared throughout other people's lives, and we question how come the fruits are not baring out of our own lives.

We want to reap the blessings but don't want to trust and start the process. You attract like-minded people, and if you don't like what you're attracting, you have to change the mindset you have about yourself. A winning mindset requires you to surround yourself with other winners. God showed me a vision at 13 that I would travel throughout and bring a message of hope and assurance to my generation. At 13, I have seen through visions that I will be a motivational speaker, author, and educator, helping others break obstacles and chains so they can walk into their full purpose. At 13, I saw myself speaking at big conferences and being a keynote speaker in the heart of my city and also for the city that I grew up in. At 13, I have seen myself speaking in front of legislation and talking about things that need change that is impacting the community. I have seen all this at 13.

Because of what I saw through visions, I firmly believed with everything within me that this was my purpose in speaking. I didn't know when this was going to happen or how it was going to happen, but I knew I had a duty to be willing to be stretched for good. I know I had to be willing to do what made me uncomfortable. I know I had to change some things so what I am called to do can manifest.

I know I had to be willing to go through the process to change my circle, or else my circle would change me. The book of life says bad company ruins good character. If I don't change what I was attracting before I knew it, I will start reaping the actions those around me will be reaping. I had to change what I was speaking in order for me to change how I was thinking. A broken mindset gives broken responses, but a victory mindset gives victory responses. I had to change what I was declaring in the atmosphere in order for me to attract what I wanted to attract. I started declaring the I cans in life, and I started to focus on the I cans in life and just believed that this would manifest. All of a sudden, opportunity after opportunity arose for me to get my feet wet and expand to do what God showed me at 13. I was attracting people into my circle who were the best at what they did.

I was able to learn from the best in the field I wanted to get into. I had Les Brown as my mentor, who taught me what I needed to know to be the best at what I do. I learned from Earl Thomas, who taught me how to execute and put into action. He taught me how to want it as badly as I wanted to breathe. There were great leaders and icons that I learned from. Because I learned from the best, I landed my first speaking engagement at 17 years old.

It was my senior year in high school when I was sent to Kansas City, Missouri, to speak at a big national conference called ASHA (American School Health Association), where I spoke in front of hundreds of doctors, lawyers, teachers, nurses, focusing on the disparities in our education system and how it impacts the community. I was one of 4 youth presenters from Washington State to speak at this big national conference.

Afterward, I was able to be the keynote speaker for the 20th year anniversary of the city of SeaTac, located in WA. I was talking about my story of being in the city, growing up in the city, and the impact it had on me. I didn't look for these opportunities, these opportunities came to my door, and I took them. I was able to speak in front of the heart of Seattle right after the Florida school shooting, where 400-plus kids walked out and protested due to the rise of school shootings.

I was bringing a message of hope and assurance with Mike Wansley, better known by his stage name as Wanz, who was featured on the song "Thrift Shop" with Macklemore. At that moment, I found myself being the voice for my generation that will bring a message of the impact that will motivate others to move in action. Who are you surrounding yourself with? Are they holding you back from elevating to the next level? If your circle is not elevating you or pushing you, then you're in the wrong circle. So many times, we stay where we are because we are comfortable where we are. However, in order to have a winning mindset and start executing, it's going to require us to change our circle, change the affirmations that we declare, fight until we can't fight anymore, and the last part it's going to require us to believe.

Believe

Believing is the foundation behind everything. You can do steps 1-3, but if you don't have to believe that it will happen for you, there's no point in doing steps 1-3. When I was featured on Yahoo Finance with Ice Cube, the first question people asked me was, Josias, how do you do it? Josias, what did you do? I told them I let go and I let God, I believed what God showed me at the age of 13, and I executed from there.

When I was featured on LA Wire 30 under 30, with Lil Nas X and Arianna Grandè, people asked me what the secret was. They tell me they do steps 1-3; however, they are not bearing any fruit. While going through the process and explaining to these individuals, the main question I asked them was, what do you believe about yourself? What do you say about yourself? When you look at the mirror, what do you see in the mirror? Steps 1-3 have no seed if you don't believe in the positive about yourself.

They tell me that they don't believe it, but they just do it to do it. A winning mindset requires you to believe in the possible even when you think it may be impossible. What do you mean? God is the God of purpose, and he's also the God of victory, and what God says about us is far more important than what the world says about us. When you want to win, you have to have the lens of possibilities and not the lens of impossibilities. The impossible only see defeat and an impossible outcome, but the possible lens sees the possibilities in every outcome. The difference between the two impossible vs. I'm possible is the lens eye view of how one sees it. One will determine the lens based on what they have declared over their lives, what they believe about themselves, and who they are surrounding themselves with.

The impossible lens doesn't see the good coming out of anything, but the possible lens sees the good coming out of everything. The impossible lens is the lens of the world, but then I'm possible lens is the lens of Christ. What do you mean? No matter how big the storm might be in life, no matter the trials and tribulations we face, God always sees the best in us no matter what. When everyone else around us may see the worst, God sees the best.

If the God of purpose who created each and every one of us sees the possibilities, why do we see the impossibilities? People saw an individual who stuttered, was in special ed, English second language, talked too fast, and could barely comprehend, and based on that, people deemed my life goals and dreams as impossible. They have seen the limitations and said this would never happen. Educators told me to throw in the towel, and people tried to persuade me to give up and to stop believing that I would ever be someone of influence. I had a choice to either believe that my goals would not happen or believe through it all that my goals would flourish. I had a choice to believe that it was possible or to believe that it was impossible. I chose to believe and download what God said about me and what God showed me. So despite what was happening to me, I chose to believe something good would manifest. I chose to believe that God could turn it around for good.

A winning mindset requires you to believe there will be a way out, even though it may seem like there's no way out. A winning mindset requires you to not see what you're in through the lens of the impossible but see what you're in through the lens of the possible. You're made to win, and no matter what happens, your story is a jewel to someone else. Your life testimony is a lifeline to someone else's healing. You're not an accident; you're here for a purpose on purpose and with a purpose. Through it, all win, and make sure you stay standing.

Made in the USA
Monee, IL
07 June 2023

35283375R00085